A Practical Guide to Alternative Assessment

Joan L. Herman
Pamela R. Aschbacher
Lynn Winters

Association for Supervision
and Curriculum Development

Association for Supervision and Curriculum Development
1250 N. Pitt St., Alexandria, VA 22314
(703) 549-9110

This work was supported under the Educational Research and Development Center Program cooperative agreement R117G10027 and CFDA catalog number 84.117G as administered by the Office of Educational Research and Improvement, U.S. Department of Education. The findings and opinions expressed in this work do not reflect the position or policies of the Office of Educational Research and Improvement or the U.S. Department of Education.

Printed in the United States of America.

Ronald S. Brandt, *Executive Editor*
Nancy Modrak, *Managing Editor, Books*
Ginger R. Miller, *Associate Editor*
Gary Bloom, *Manager, Design and Production Services*
Keith Demmons, *Cover Design*
Valerie Sprague, *Desktop Typesetter*

Price: $10.95
ASCD Stock Number: 611-92140
ISBN: 0-87120-197-6

Library of Congress Cataloging-in-Publication Data

Herman, Joan L.
    A practical guide to alternative assessment / Joan L. Herman.
    Pamela R. Aschbacher, Lynn Winters.
      p.   cm.
    Includes bibliographical references.
    ISBN 0-87120-197-6
    1. Educational tests and measurements—United States.
    I. Aschbacher, Pamela R. II. Winters, Lynn. III. Title.
    LB3051.H45   1992
    371.2′7′0973—dc20   92-30244
                                                    CIP

A Practical Guide to Alternative Assessment

Foreword

The caveat "Not everything that counts can be counted and not everything that can be counted counts" was reportedly posted on Albert Einstein's office wall. In the context of present educational reform discussions, this almost prophetic statement has implications for the assessment of student learning.

Assessment has become the focus of our nation's current educational reform agenda. Although our dialogue on authentic assessment has been elevated beyond the measurement of purely quantifiable or "countable" demonstrations of complex human performances, we have lacked a comprehensive, systematic, and integrated framework to assist practitioners in designing and developing alternative assessments.

In *A Practical Guide to Alternative Assessment*, Joan Herman, Pamela Aschbacher, and Lynn Winters offer cogent guidance on the creation and use of alternative measures of student achievement. They present a systematic, integrative, and iterative process model that links assessment with curriculum and instruction, based on contemporary theories of learning and cognition.

The authors review the purposes of assessment and provide a substantive rationale for alternative structures. Yet, as they point out, the heart of the book is the illumination of several key assessment issues that reaffirm our knowledge that assessment tasks must be informed by the most important elements of instructional practice. These issues include:

1. Assessment must be congruent with significant instructional goals.

2. Assessment must involve the examination of the processes as well as the products of learning.

3. Performance-based activities do not constitute assessment per se.

4. Cognitive learning theory and its constructivist approach to knowledge acquisition supports the need to integrate assessment methodologies with instructional outcomes and curriculum content.

5. An integrated and active view of student learning requires the assessment of holistic and complex performance.

6. Assessment design is dependent on assessment purpose; grading and monitoring student progress are distinct from diagnosis and improvement.

7. The key to effective assessment is the match between the task and the intended student outcome.

8. The criteria used to evaluate student performance are critical; in the absence of criteria, assessment remains an isolated and episodic activity.

9. Quality assessment provides substantive data for making informed decisions about student learning.

10. Assessment systems that provide the most comprehensive feedback on student growth include multiple measures taken over time.

The word "assess" comes from the French "assidere," which means "to sit beside." By clarifying the critical conceptual and technical aspects of using alternative assessments, the authors have reaffirmed the fundamental role of assessment, which is to provide authentic and meaningful feedback for improving student learning, instructional practice, and educational options.

As the authors state, assessment is not an end in itself. It is a process that facilitates appropriate instructional decision making by providing information on two fundamental questions: How are we doing? and How can we do it better?

Perhaps the best way to answer those questions is to sit beside the learner and find out. Now that's an interesting alternative!

STEPHANIE PACE MARSHALL
ASCD President, 1992–93

1

■

Rethinking Assessment

Assessment is a cornerstone of education reform in the '90s: the President's education agenda, America 2000; the National Education Goals set by the governors; concerns for international competitiveness; renewed calls for restructuring and accountability at the state, local, and school levels. These potent, highly visible initiatives ask educators and the nation to focus on high-level goals for our children. They ask that we set our sights on excellence and track our progress toward attaining it for individual students, for schools, for districts, for states, and for the nation. Requiring us to assess progress, they often pose assessment itself as a key to attaining such progress, thus ensuring assessment's priority status in schools.

Yet this heightened emphasis on assessment comes at a time of growing dissatisfaction with traditional, multiple-choice forms of testing. The result is an explosion of interest in alternative forms of assessment combined with attempts across the country at all levels—national, state, local, and classroom—to create them. Talk of portfolios, exhibits, hands-on experiments, and writing-across-the-curriculum abounds. Despite numerous conferences and meetings on these topics, educators have had little concrete guidance in the creation and use of alternative assessments.

This book is intended to contribute to the process of creating alternative forms of assessment. It is written for preservice and practicing teachers, school administrators, and district- and state-level practitioners who are interested in developing new kinds of assessments. Based on current views of meaningful learning and curriculum as well as both established and evolving principles of measurement quality, this book provides a systematic approach to assessment design and raises issues critical to ensuring high-quality assessments. In this introductory chapter, we provide background on the purposes of assessment and the need for new alternatives, plus an overview of the key assessment development issues, which constitute the heart of the book.

It is important to note also what this book is not intended to do. It is not meant as a primer on how to plan and implement a comprehensive assessment system or on how to mount a total classroom assessment program. We emphasize key concerns in developing a single, good assessment, one crucial ingredient for sound assessment practices.

Clarifying Terms

Many terms are advanced when discussing alternatives to conventional, multiple-choice testing. These include alternative assessment, authentic assessment, and performance-based assessment. We use these terms synonymously to mean variants of performance assessments that require students to generate rather than choose a response. Performance assessment by any name requires students to actively accomplish complex and significant tasks, while bringing to bear prior knowledge, recent learning, and relevant skills to solve realistic or authentic problems. Exhibitions, investigations, demonstrations, written or oral responses, journals, and portfolios are examples of the assessment alternatives we think of when we use the term "alternative assessment."

Understanding the Promise of Assessment

Why all the attention to testing and other assessments? Why do we need them? Assessment serves needs at all levels of the education hierarchy; for example, assessment helps educators set standards, create instruction pathways, motivate performance, provide diagnostic feedback, assess/evaluate progress, and communicate progress to others.

Whether we are teachers giving routine exams in our classrooms or policymakers mandating achievement tests, through testing we set and communicate *standards* to those around us: We tell them what's important, what deserves focus, and what we expect as good performance. In the process, significant stakes are often associated with test results—classroom grades, college admission decisions, job security, self-satisfaction, and other perks—thus motivating performance. We not only communicate to students what's important by including a subject in a classroom test, we are also motivating students to learn it. Policymakers who mandate tests are suggesting what we should emphasize in the schools and are motivating us and our students to perform well on their tests.

Similarly, feedback and progress monitoring functions of assessment work at several levels. For administrators and school planners, test results provide information about program effectiveness and identify areas of curricular strength and weakness. In so doing they prove useful for resource allocation, for identifying staff development or materials needs, and for targeting and assessing plans for improvement. For teachers, testing provides important diagnostic information for instructional groupings, for identifying instructional needs and prescribing appropriate instruction, for determining mastery, and for assessing the effectiveness of particular instructional units or approaches. For parents and students, testing information is a gauge of individual progress, which helps them understand and build on individual strengths and weaknesses.

For all, testing promises to answer the questions: *"How am I [are we] doing?" "How can I [we] do better?"*

Testing fulfills its promise only if it meets some critical conditions. Chief among these is the meaning of test performance: tests are useful and productive to the extent that they represent *significant* outcomes for students and the important goals of classroom instruction. In other words, to be valid, fair, and useful, test content must match the knowledge, skills, and dispositions that teachers are teaching and those that students are expected to learn or acquire.

Figure 1.1 is a simple model illustrating how assessment information can be used systematically to support and facilitate instructional improvement. As the figure shows, schools and teachers generally synthesize data from many sources to arrive at school or class goals for students. These sources include societal expectations, state and district curriculum frameworks, legal requirements, and available texts and other instructional materials, along with professional standards and professional judgments. Once defined, these goals or outcomes serve as guideposts for designing instruction and assessment. Because they reflect the same goals that direct instructional activities, assessment results guide instructional planning and serve as measures of instructional effective-

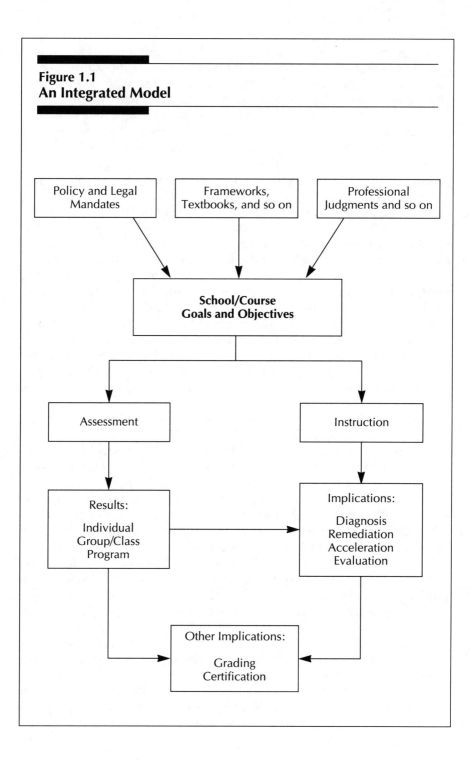

Figure 1.1
An Integrated Model

ness. Assessment results can be used to identify areas where individuals may need more help, where additional class instruction is needed, where instructional units can be improved, where staff development resources need to be targeted, and so forth. When instruction and assessment are linked to a common set of *significant* learning goals, assessments make sense and can be used to improve instruction.

It is not that tests ought to drive the curriculum, or that teachers ought to teach to the test. Rather, *good assessment*[1] *is an integral part of good instruction.* Both testing and instruction ought to reflect significant, agreed on goals for students. Assessments should *measure* important classroom objectives; assessment results should represent how students perform on the broad knowledge and skill domains reflected by those objectives; and classroom instruction should provide students with the opportunity to learn and attain the knowledge and skills.

Understanding the Limitations of Conventional Assessment

Recent criticisms raise questions about the fit between the model shown in Figure 1.1 and existing testing practices. Do test scores represent significant learning outcomes? Do improvements in test score performance actually represent improvements in learning (Cannell 1987, Linn et al. 1990, Shepard 1989)? How is it possible that nearly all states report scoring "above average" compared to a national norm group? The whole notion of "average" in comparison to a nationally representative norm group suggests that some will score below, some at, and some above average. Are improvements in test scores the result of improved teaching and learning, or do they reflect a meager curriculum with students being "drilled and killed" on expected test content?

The litany goes on. Many people question whether current standardized tests adequately represent important goals for student learning and development. Criticisms include the narrowness of test content that concentrates principally on basic skills in reading, language, and math; the mismatch between test content and curriculum and instruction; the overemphasis on routine and discrete skills with a neglect of complex thinking and problem solving; and the limited relevance of multiple-

---

[1]While testing and assessment are used more or less synonymously in this book, we tend to favor the term assessment because it encourages us to think beyond traditional definitions of testing.

choice formats to either classroom or real-world learning (Baker 1989, Shepard 1989, Herman and Golan 1990). Can educational programs guided by typical, standardized, multiple-choice testing produce meaningful outcomes? Critics of testing think not.

Considering Alternatives

Dissatisfaction with existing standardized testing coupled with unabated faith in the value of systematic assessment have given rise to proposals for new assessment alternatives. Whether we call these alternatives performance testing, authentic assessment, portfolio assessment, process testing, exhibits, or demonstrations, the hope is that they will better capture significant and enduring educational outcomes. While proposed assessment strategies may be diverse, they share a common vision (see Figure 1.2).

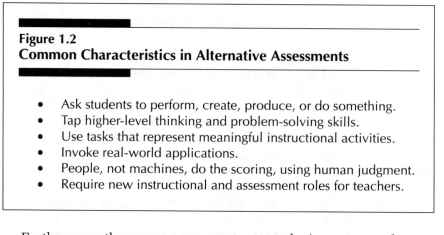

Figure 1.2
Common Characteristics in Alternative Assessments

- Ask students to perform, create, produce, or do something.
- Tap higher-level thinking and problem-solving skills.
- Use tasks that represent meaningful instructional activities.
- Invoke real-world applications.
- People, not machines, do the scoring, using human judgment.
- Require new instructional and assessment roles for teachers.

Furthermore, these new assessments stress the importance of examining the p*rocesses* as well as the products of learning. They encourage us to move beyond the "one right answer" mentality and to challenge students to explore the possibilities inherent in open-ended, complex problems, and to draw their own inferences.

Figure 1.3 shows the range of assessment alternatives currently being discussed. While some are being heralded as new alternatives, they actually represent assessment techniques and issues that teachers have dealt with for years. Good teachers are always attuned to the process of instruction—how a lesson is going, who's having difficulty, who's paying attention, how a certain group is working—and adjust their instructional plans and activities accordingly. Similarly, most teachers use a range of information sources to determine how well their students have learned. What is new about these assessments is that they make explicit and formal what was previously implicit and informal. They also encourage teachers to articulate their instructional goals clearly, to ensure alignment between their goals and current views of meaningful teaching and learning, and to gather systematic evidence to guide their instructional efforts.

Figure 1.3
Assessment Alternatives

Assessing Processes	Assessing Products
• Clinical interviews	• Essays with prompts and scoring criteria
• Documented observations	• Projects with rating criteria
• Student learning logs and journals	• Student portfolios with rating criteria
• Student self-evaluation (oral or written)	• Student demonstrations/ investigations (expository or using the arts)
• Debriefing interviews about student projects, products, and demonstrations (student explains what, why, and how, and reflects on possible changes	• Paintings, drama, dances, and stories with rating criteria
• Behavioral checklists	• Attitude inventories, surveys
• Student think-alouds in conjunction with standardized or multiple-choice tests	• Standardized or multiple-choice tests, perhaps with section for "explanations"

Supporting Instructional Improvement

Direct assessment of student writing illustrates the potential power of these new types of assessments: the integration of instruction and assessment. In one district, teachers collaborated to define the attributes of good writing and developed a scoring scheme to capture the attributes. Other teachers were then trained in the reliable use of the scoring scheme and were used as raters in a districtwide writing assessment. Teachers found that the elements of the scoring rubric provided a good anchor for their instruction and gave them a fast and uniform way to assess and provide feedback for their students' classroom writing. Furthermore, the district's emphasis on writing and other state initiatives encouraged the teachers to change some aspects of their writing instruction. The result was improved student writing and teacher confidence in their instruction and assessment. The development of performance tests in other content areas, with similar support for instructional change, shows similar promise.

Knowing How to Proceed
with Assessment Development

Although alternative assessment implies new strategies for looking at educational outcomes, the process for developing these assessments is based on decades of measurement research. Developers of high-quality tests, be they norm-referenced, criterion-referenced, or performance-based tests, adhere to the following process with certain variations:

1. Specify the nature of the skills and accomplishments students are to develop.

2. Specify illustrative tasks that would require students to demonstrate these skills and accomplishments.

3. Specify the criteria and standards for judging student performance on the task.

4. Develop a reliable rating process.

5. Gather evidence of validity to show what kinds of inferences can be made from the assessment.

6. Use test results to refine assessment and improve curriculum and instruction; provide feedback to students, parents, and the community.

Subsequent chapters describe how this test development process applies to alternative assessment. The process itself is modified according to an assessment's purpose, no matter the format of assessment. For example, with large-scale assessment or minimum competency testing where stakes are high and one-shot assessment is typical, all steps are essential. For routine classroom assessment, when teachers have continual opportunities to formally or informally assess student progress, steps four and five are less crucial. In the classroom, the results of any single assessment are moderated by other forms of formal and informal evidence; this compensates for what may be lost by not gathering formal validity and reliability data. Nonetheless, teachers need to be well-acquainted with the characteristics of a technically sound assessment process so they can be wise consumers of the large-scale assessments and commercial products that influence their classroom practices.

Balancing Assessment Strategies

There is no one right way to assess students. Although we present a strong case for performance assessment, we neither say that all assessments need to be of this type nor reject the use of multiple-choice and other forms of selected- response tests. We do affirm that performance assessments offer appealing ways to assess complex thinking and problem-solving skills and, because they are grounded in realistic problems, are potentially more motivating and reinforcing for students. However, while performance assessments may tell us how well and deeply students can apply their knowledge, multiple-choice tests may be more efficient for determining how well students have acquired the basic facts and concepts. A balanced curriculum requires a balanced approach to assessment.

Furthermore, just because an assessment asks students to perform an interesting or complex activity does not make it a good assessment. Good assessment reliably *measures* something beyond the specific tasks that students are asked to complete. The results of good assessment identify what students can do in a broad knowledge or skill domain. The skills that students exhibit in the assessment situation should transfer to other situations and other problems.

Holding Assessments to High Standards

Regardless of the purpose or format, quality assessments should meet certain common standards. The Center for Research on Evaluation, Standards, and Student Testing (CRESST), (Linn, Baker, and Dunbar 1991) has developed criteria that represent a touchstone throughout the assessment development process. The criteria include:

- **Consequences.** Testing history is full of examples of good intentions gone awry. This criterion requires that we plan from the outset to assess the actual consequences of the assessment. Does it have positive consequences or are there unintended effects such as narrowing of curriculum, adverse effects on disadvantaged students, and so on?

- **Fairness.** Does the assessment consider fairly the cultural background of those students taking the test? Have all students had equal opportunity to learn the complex thinking and problem-solving skills that are being targeted?

- **Transfer and Generalizability.** Will the assessment results support accurate generalizations about student capability? Are the results reliable across raters, and consistent in meaning across locales?

- **Cognitive Complexity.** We cannot tell from simply looking at an assessment whether or not it actually assesses complex thinking skills. Does an assessment in fact *require* students to use complex thinking and problem solving?

- **Content Quality.** The tasks selected to measure a given content domain should themselves be worthy of students' and raters' time and efforts. Is the selected content consistent with the best current understanding of the field and does it reflect important aspects of a discipline that will stand the test of time?

- **Content Coverage.** The content coverage criterion requires that assessment be aligned with the curriculum and, over a set of assessments, represent the full curriculum. Because time constraints will probably limit the number of alternative assessments that can be given, adequate content coverage represents a significant challenge. Are the key elements of the curriculum covered by the set of assessments?

- **Meaningfulness.** One of the rationales for more contextualized assessments is that they ensure that students engage in meaningful problems that result in worthwhile educational experiences and higher levels of motivation. Do students find the assessment tasks realistic and worthwhile?

- **Cost and Efficiency.** To be effective tools, assessments must be cost effective. Labor-intensive performance-based assessments require efficient data collection and scoring procedures. Is the information about students worth the cost and time to obtain it?

Finally, it is important to note that alternative assessment is a developing field. New strategies are evolving as are new methodologies for ensuring their quality. As we learn more about alternative assessment, current approaches may be refined or even reformulated.

References

Baker, E.L. (1989). "Mandated Tests: Educational Reform or Quality Indicator?" In *Test Policy and Test Performance: Education, Language, and Culture*, edited by B.R. Gifford. (pp. 3-23). Norwell, Mass.: Kluwer.

Cannell, J.J. (1987). *Nationally Normed Elementary Achievement Testing in America's Public Schools: How all 50 States Are Above the National Average.* (2nd ed.). Daniels, W. Va.: Friends of Education.

Herman J., and S. Golan. (1990). *Effects of Standardized Testing on Teachers and Learning: Another Look.* (Tech. Rep. No. 334). Los Angeles: University of California, Center for the Study of Evaluation.

Linn, R.L., E.L. Baker, and S.B. Dunbar. (1991). "Complex, Performance-based Assessment: Expectations and Validation Criteria." *Educational Researcher* 20, 8: 15-23.

Linn, R.L., M.E. Graue, and N.M. Sanders. (1990). *Comparing State and District Test Results to National Norms: Interpretations of Scoring "Above the National Average."* (CSE Tech. Rep. No. 308). Los Angeles: University of California, Center for the Study of Evaluation.

Shepard, L.A. (April 1989). "Why We Need Better Assessments." *Educational Leadership* 46, 7: 4-9.

2

Linking Assessment and Instruction

New visions of effective curriculum, instruction, and learning demand new attention to systematic assessment. No longer is learning thought to be a one-way transmission from teacher to students with the teacher as lecturer and students as passive receptacles. Rather, meaningful instruction engages students actively in the learning process. Good teachers draw on and synthesize discipline-based knowledge, knowledge of student learning, and knowledge of child development. They use a variety of instructional strategies, from direct instruction to coaching, to involve their students in meaningful activities-discussion, group process, hands-on projects—and to achieve specific learning goals. Good teachers constantly assess how their students are doing, gather evidence of problems and progress, and adjust their instructional plans accordingly.

In this chapter we review the educational and societal trends that support these new visions of teaching and learning, which have led to a need for new forms of assessment (see Figure 2.1). These same trends place unprecedented demands on teachers' professional skills, requiring them to integrate knowledge of intended goals, learning processes, curriculum content, and assessment.

Figure 2.1
Recent Trends in Assessment

1. Changes from behavioral to cognitive views of learning and assessment

   - From sole emphasis on the products or outcomes of student learning to a concern for the learning process
   - From passive response to active construction of meaning
   - From assessment of discrete, isolated skills to integrated and cross-disciplinary assessment
   - Attention to metacognition (self-monitoring and learning to learn skills) and conative skills (motivation and other areas of affect that influence learning and achievement)
   - Changes in the meaning of knowing and being skilled—from an accumulation of isolated facts and skills to an emphasis on the application and use of knowledge.

2. From paper-pencil to authentic assessment

   - Relevance and meaningfulness to students
   - Contextualized problems
   - Emphasis on complex skills
   - Not single correct answer
   - Public standards, known in advance
   - Individual pacing and growth.

3. Portfolios: from single occasion assessment to samples over time

   - Basis for assessment by teacher
   - Basis for self assessment by students
   - Basis for assessment by parents.

4. From single attribute to multi-dimensional assessments

   - Recognition of students' many abilities and talents
   - Growing recognition of the malleability of student ability
   - Opportunities for students to develop and exhibit diverse abilities.

5. From near exclusive emphasis on individual assessment to group assessment

   - Group process skills
   - Collaborative products.

Facing New Demands on Education

Consider what futurists' predictions imply for educational goals and for the kinds of skills students and society as a whole will need for the 21st century (Benjamin 1989). Knowledge is exploding geometrically; the world's knowledge base has quadrupled in this century (Cornish 1986). Given this pace, no one individual can be expected to keep up with the information flow in a single discipline, much less across disciplines. Such a knowledge explosion makes futile most attempts to have students memorize and regurgitate large bodies of facts.

Economic trends also push us away from a fact-based curriculum. The shift from a manufacturing- to an information- and service-based economy requires that individuals have skills in accessing and using information and in working with people. These changes in the workforce and in the pace and complexity of modern life suggest that people will need to be flexible, to shift jobs frequently, and to adapt to change. To prepare students for success in the future, schools must emphasize how to apply rather than just acquire information.

Using Cognitive Learning Theories

New cognitive theories of learning propel us in similar directions. Early learning theories assumed that complex skills were acquired bit-by-bit in a carefully arranged sequence of small prerequisite and component skills, often articulated in discrete behavioral objectives. It was assumed that rote basic skills should be taught and mastered before going on to "higher-order," complex thinking skills. Evidence from contemporary cognitive psychology, however, indicates that learning is not linear and is not acquired by assembling bits of simpler learning. Learning is an ongoing process during which students are continually receiving information, interpreting it, connecting it to what they already know and have experienced (their prior knowledge), and reorganizing and revising their internal conceptions of the world, which are called "mental models," "knowledge structures," or "schema."

Learning's Active Nature

From today's cognitive perspective, meaningful learning is reflective, constructive, and self-regulated (Wittrock 1991, Bransford and Vye 1989,

Marzano et al. 1988, Davis et al. 1990). People do not merely record factual information but create their own unique understandings of the world—their own knowledge structures. To *know* something is not just to passively receive information, but to interpret it and incorporate it into one's prior knowledge. In addition, we now recognize the importance of knowing not just how to perform, but also when to perform and how to adapt that performance to new situations. The presence or absence of discrete bits of information, which is typically the focus of many traditional multiple-choice tests, is not of primary importance in the assessment of meaningful learning. Instead, we care more about how and whether students organize, structure, and use that information in context to solve complex problems.

Learning Is Not Linear

Learning does not best proceed in discrete hierarchies. Because learning is not linear and can take many directions at once at an uneven pace, conceptual learning is not something to be delayed until a particular age or until all the "basic facts" have been mastered. People of all ages and ability levels constantly use and refine concepts.

Current evidence makes it clear that instruction emphasizing structured drill and practice on isolated facts and skills does students a major disservice. Insisting that students demonstrate a certain level of arithmetic mastery before being allowed to enroll in algebra or that they learn how to write a good paragraph before tackling an essay are examples of this discrete skills approach. Such learning out of context makes it more difficult to organize and remember the information being presented. Applying taught skills later when solving real-world problems also becomes more difficult. Students who have trouble mastering decontextualized "basics" are often put in remedial classes or groups and are not given the opportunity to tackle complex and meaningful tasks.

Learners Are Multitalented

Current intelligence theories that stress the existence of a variety of human talents and capabilities depart from the popular view that intelligence or ability is a single, fixed capability (Sternberg 1991, Gardner 1982). Gardner argues that while traditional schooling has emphasized only two abilities, verbal-linguistic and logical-mathematical, many other important "intelligences" exist, including visual-spatial, kinesthetic, musical, intrapersonal, and interpersonal. Gardner claims that all individuals have strengths in two or three of these areas. Furthermore, a tremendous variety exists in the modes and speeds with which people acquire knowledge, in the attention and memory capabilities they can apply to knowledge acquisition and performance, and in the ways in which they can demonstrate the personal meaning they have created. To be successful with all students, instruction and assessment need to draw on more than linguistic or logical-mathematical intelligences and subscribe to the assumption that *all* students can learn.

Learning Includes Cognition, Metacognition, and Affect

Recent studies of the integration of learning and motivation highlight the importance of affective and metacognitive (thinking about thinking) skills in learning (McCombs 1991, Weinstein and Meyer 1991). For example, Belmont and others (1982) suggest that poor thinkers and problem solvers differ from good ones not so much in the skills they possess as in their failure to use the skills. Mere acquisition of knowledge and skills does not make people into competent thinkers or problem solvers. They must also acquire the disposition to use the skills and strategies and know when to apply them.

Research and experience, such as that in the writing field (Gere and Stevens 1985, Burnham 1986), demonstrate the value of engaging learners in thoughtful consideration of what constitutes excellent work and how to judge their own efforts. Providing students with models of exemplary performance and encouraging them to reflect on their work helps students to understand and internalize high standards.

Meaningful learning is seen as intrinsically motivating. The long-term value of traditional, extrinsic motivators such as grades and stars is questionable. Research suggests that these techniques may even detract from a learner's intrinsic motivation, resulting in lowered mastery or performance (Lepper and Greene 1978).

Learning's Social Context

The role of the social context in shaping complex cognitive abilities and dispositions has also received attention over the past several years. Although real-life problems often require people to work together as a group, most traditional instruction and assessment have involved independent work. We now know that groups facilitate learning in several ways. Working together with peers on a common task provides: (1) many models of effective thinking strategies; (2) mutual constructive feedback; (3) an appreciation for the value of collaborating with others; and (4) help in attaining difficult or complex skills or knowledge.

The demands of a democracy provide other rationales for the value of group inquiry. Students who work together in a "community of learners" are expected to listen to each other with respect, to reflect and build on one another's ideas, to demand evidence to support opinions, to assist each other in drawing implications, and to challenge the facts, assumptions, and arguments of different points of view (Jones and Fennimore 1990).

Focusing on a Thinking Curriculum

A modern approach to curriculum, coined the "Thinking Curriculum" by Lauren Resnick and Leopold Klopfer (1989), strongly advocates an integrated, active view of student learning. The thinking curriculum stresses the importance of process as well as product. Students are often involved in tasks similar to those encountered in the real world. Students carry out tasks requiring complex thinking, planning, and evaluating. They solve problems, make decisions, construct arguments, and so forth. In this way, they model the process of a professional discipline while acquiring knowledge in that discipline.

According to Fennimore and Tinzmann (1990), the following four key principles characterize a thinking curriculum.

Promotion of In-depth Learning

A thinking curriculum helps students acquire the key concepts and tools for making, using, and communicating knowledge in a specific field. Working knowledge of the field implies an integrated network of knowledge and concepts rather than a collection of isolated facts.

In a thinking curriculum, students develop an in-depth understanding of the essential concepts and processes for dealing with those concepts, similar to the approach taken by experts in tackling their tasks. For example, students use original sources to construct historical accounts; they design experiments to answer their questions about natural phenomena; they use mathematics to model real-world events and systems; and they write for real audiences.

Content and Process Objectives in Real-world Tasks

Rather than focusing on simple and discrete skills, students engage in the complex, holistic thinking needed to meet challenges outside the classroom. According to Resnick (1989), such real-life thinking often involves: meaningful processes of decision making and problem solving; collaborating with others; the use of available tools; connection to real-world events and objects; and use of interdisciplinary knowledge.

Holistic Performances in Increasingly Challenging Environments

A thinking curriculum does not isolate skills and facts. Rather it includes the holistic performance of meaningful, complex tasks in increasingly challenging environments. Materials and content are structured so that students gradually regulate their own learning. This approach ensures that learning motivates students and encourages in them a sense of efficacy and confidence.

Connection of Content and Process to Learners' Backgrounds

A thinking curriculum takes into account the experiences and knowledge that students bring to school and then expands on and refines this prior knowledge by connecting it to new learning, making curriculum content relevant to important issues and tasks in the students' lives. When students relate school learning to real-life issues they are more likely to seek and value the perspectives of others—peers, teachers, parents, community members, and experts. In so doing, they develop interpersonal competencies for creating and participating in dialogue with individuals who have different perspectives and come from diverse backgrounds.

Linking Assessment and Instruction

Figure 2.2 summarizes many of the basic learning principles discussed in this chapter and describes some of the implications these principles have for both instruction and assessment. As Figure 2.2 indicates, assessment not only evaluates how much was learned in any particular unit of instruction, but also provides "real time" information to students and teachers about their progress and ways to improve.

Figure 2.2
Linking Instruction and Assessment:
Implications from Cognitive Learning Theory

Theory: Knowledge is constructed. Learning is a process of creating personal meaning from new information and prior knowledge.
    Implications for Instruction/Assessment:
- Encourage discussion of new ideas.
- Encourage divergent thinking, multiple links and solutions, not just one right answer.
- Encourage multiple modes of expression, for example, role play, simulations, debates, and explanations to others.
- Emphasize critical thinking skills: analyze, compare, generalize, predict, hypothesize.
- Relate new information to personal experience, prior knowledge.
- Apply information to a new situation.

Theory: All ages/abilities can think and solve problems. Learning isn't necessarily a linear progression of discrete skills.
    Implications for Instruction/Assessment:
- Engage all students in problem solving.
- Don't make problem solving, critical thinking, or discussion of concepts contingent on mastery of routine basic skills.

Theory: There is great variety in learning styles, attention spans, memory, developmental paces, and intelligences.
    Implications for Instruction/Assessment:
- Provide choices in tasks (not all reading and writing).
- Provide choices in how to show mastery/competence.
- Provide time to think about and do assignments.
- Don't overuse timed tests.
- Provide opportunity to revise, rethink.
- Include concrete experiences (manipulatives, links to prior personal experience).

continued

Figure 2.2—*continued*

Theory: People perform better when they know the goal, see models, know how their performance compares to the standard.
Implications for Instruction/Assessment:
- Discuss goals; let students help define them (personal and class).
- Provide a range of examples of student work; discuss characteristics.
- Provide students with opportunities for self-evaluation and peer review.
- Discuss criteria for judging performance.
- Allow students to have input into standards.

Theory: It's important to know when to use knowledge, how to adapt it, how to manage one's own learning.
Implications for Instruction/Assessment:
- Give real-world opportunities (or simulations) to apply/adapt new knowledge.
- Have students self-evaluate: think about how they learn well/poorly; set new goals, why they like certain work.

Theory: Motivation, effort, and self-esteem affect learning and performance.
Implications for Instruction/Assessment:
- Motivate students with real-life tasks and connections to personal experiences.
- Encourage students to see connection between effort and results.

Theory: Learning has social components. Group work is valuable.
Implications for Instruction/Assessment:
- Provide group work.
- Incorporate heterogeneous groups.
- Enable students to take on a variety of roles.
- Consider group products and group processes.

Assessments' various forms promote a multiplicity of goals that include, but are not limited to, the acquisition of content knowledge. Tests are no longer limited to scheduled, timed, pencil-paper tasks for individuals to perform alone to show what they know. Assessment now takes place in many contexts and includes individual and group work, aided and unaided responses, and short or long time periods. Open discussion of performance criteria and standards of excellence among teachers, students, and even parents serves as a hallmark of alternative assessment. Because assessment is an integral part of instruction, consideration of instructional goals is the crucial first step in designing meaningful assessment tasks and scoring procedures.

References

Belmont, J.M., E.C. Butterfield, and R.P. Ferretti. (1982). "To Secure Transfer of Training, Instruct Self-management Skills." In *How and How Much Can Intelligence Be Increased?* edited by D.K. Detterman and R.J. Sternberg. Norwood, N.J.: Ablex.

Benjamin, S. (1989). "An Ideascape for Education: What Futurists Recommend." *Educational Leadership* 7, 1: 8-14.

Bransford, J.D., and N. Vye. (1989). "A Perspective on Cognitive Research and its Implications in Instruction." In *Toward the Thinking Curriculum: Current Cognitive Research (1989 Yearbook of the Association for Supervision and Curriculum Development)*, edited by L.B. Resnick and L.E. Klopfer. Alexandria, Va.: Association for Supervision and Curriculum Development.

Burnham, C. (1986). "Portfolio Evaluation: Room to Breathe and Grow." In *Training the Teacher of College Composition*, edited by C. Bridges. Urbana, Ill.: National Council of Teachers of English.

Cornish, E. (1986). "Educating Children for the 21st Century." *Curriculum Review* 25, 4: 12-17.

Davis, R.B., and C. A. Maher. (1990). "Constructivist View of the Teaching of Mathematics." *Journal for Research in Mathematics Education*. Reston, Va.: National Council of Teachers of Mathematics.

Fennimore, T.F., and M.B. Tinzmann. (1990). "Restructuring to Promote Learning in America's Schools: Video Conference 2: The Thinking Curriculum." Elmhurst, Ill.: North Central Regional Educational Laboratory.

Gardner, H. (1982). *Art, Mind and Brain*. New York: Basic Books.

Gere, A., and R. Stevens. (1985). "The Language of Writing Groups: How Oral Response Shapes Revision." In *The Acquisition of Written Language: Response & Revision*, edited by S.W. Freedman.

Jones, B.F., and T.F. Fennimore. (1990). *The New Definition of Learning: The First Step to School Reform*. Chicago: North Central Regional Educational Laboratory.

Lepper, M.R., and D. Greene. (1978). *The Hidden Costs of Reward: New Perspectives on the Psychology of Human Motivation*. Hillsdale, N.J.: Lawrence Erlbaum Associates.

Marzano, R., R. Brandt, and C.S. Hughes. (1988). *Dimensions of Thinking: A Framework for Curriculum and Instruction*. Alexandria, Va.: Association for Supervision and Curriculum Development.

McCombs, B.L. (1991). "The Definition and Measurement of Primary Motivational Processes." In *Testing and Cognition*, edited by M.C. Wittrock and E.L. Baker. Englewood Cliffs, N.J.: Prentice-Hall.

Resnick, L.B., and L.E. Klopfer. (1989). "Toward the Thinking Curriculum: An Overview." In *Toward the Thinking Curriculum: Current Cognitive Research (1989 Yearbook of the Association for Supervision and Curriculum Development)*, edited by L.B. Resnick and L.E. Klopfer. Alexandria, Va.: ASCD.

Sternberg, R.J. (1991). "Toward Better Intelligence Tests." In *Testing and Cognition*, edited by M.C. Wittrock and E.L. Baker. Englewood Cliffs, N.J.: Prentice-Hall.

Weinstein, C.E., and D.K. Meyer. (1991). "Implications of Cognitive Psychology for Testing: Contributions from Work in Learning Strategies." In *Testing and Cognition*, edited by M.C. Wittrock and E.L. Baker. Englewood Cliffs, N.J.: Prentice-Hall.

Wittrock, M.C. (1991) "Testing and Recent Research in Cognition." In *Testing and Cognition*, edited by M.C. Wittrock and E.L. Baker. Englewood Cliffs, N.J.: Prentice-Hall.

3

■

Determining Purpose

The first step in assessment design or selection is to know the purpose of your assessment: What do you plan to use the results for? What aspects of student performance do you want to know about?

While this book is not intended as a primer on the purposes and uses of assessment, you will need to consider your purpose throughout the assessment process. Is your primary purpose to assess student accomplishment—for instance, how well have students learned to write stories, to communicate orally, to synthesize research? If so, you will be most interested in assessing the status or level of student accomplishment for purposes of grading, special placement, and progress monitoring, or for school, district, and other extra-school purposes of evaluation and accountability. Because the primary intent is to describe the extent to which students have attained particular knowledge and skills, your assessment should focus on the outcomes or product of student learning.

However, if your purpose is diagnosis and improvement, such as diagnosing a student's strengths and weaknesses, prescribing the most appropriate instructional programs, or identifying strategies students use well and those they need help with, you'll want an assessment that gives you information about the process as well as the outcome. What have the students achieved and how did they do it? Process information provides such explanations.

The purpose and use of your assessment influence how much attention you give to collecting evidence of reliability and validity, a topic we treat more fully in Chapters 6 and 7. The higher the assessment stakes are, the greater the obligation to document reliability and validity. Adequate levels of both are essential when results are to be used to determine, for instance, students' promotions or placement into special classes, or to reward teachers or schools.

Setting Primary Instructional Goals

Good assessment demands that you know and are able to articulate your major instructional goals. These determine what aspects of performance you will want to know about. What do you want your students to be able to accomplish in a unit, in a course, in a discipline, or across disciplines? What should your instructional program add up to? What should students be able to do at the completion of a unit, a course, or a year of study that they were not able to do before? What critical areas of student development do you want to influence?

The answers to these questions define your classroom priorities and represent the primary targets of your instructional activities. These same priorities should also ground the assessment tasks you require of students. Such a fit contributes to a fair assessment—students have the opportunity to acquire the knowledge and skills you are assessing-and contributes to a *meaningful* assessment task that reinforces the skills and accomplishments you deem most important.

Determining Priority Outcomes

While designating goals may seem simple, it is challenging to set priorities from among the myriad possibilities. What major fields of knowledge, skills, and dispositions are worth teaching and worth assessing? What outcomes are you trying to achieve? Because performance assessments require considerable time and energy—both yours and your students—you will want to focus on a relatively small number of important outcomes, each perhaps representing a month or a quarter's worth of instruction. These assessments should aim at your major learning objectives for students. To help define these objectives, ask yourself this series of interrelated questions (to which we have supplied some sample responses):

1. What Important Cognitive Skills Do I Want My Students To Develop?
I want students to be able to:

- Communicate effectively in writing, or more specifically, to write persuasively, to write good descriptions, and to write stories.
- Communicate effectively orally.
- Analyze literature using plot, character, setting, and theme.
- Analyze issues using primary source and reference materials.
- Use algebra to solve everyday problems.
- Analyze current events from historical, political, geographic, and multicultural perspectives.
- Design and conduct studies to aid decision making about current or everyday problems.
- Use the scientific method.
- Use different media to express what they know.

2. What Social and Affective Skills Do I Want My Students To Develop?
I want them to be able to:

- Work independently.
- Develop a spirit of teamwork and skill in group work.
- Appreciate their individual strengths.
- Be persistent in the face of challenges.
- Have pride in their work.
- Enjoy and value learning.
- Have confidence in their abilities.
- Have a healthy skepticism about current arguments and claims.
- Understand that we all have strengths and that each person is able to excel in some way.

3. What Metacognitive Skills Do I Want My Students To Develop?
I want them to be able to:

- Reflect on the writing process they use, evaluate its effectiveness, and derive their own plans for how it can be improved.
- Discuss and evaluate their problem-solving strategies.
- Formulate efficient plans for completing their independent projects and for monitoring their progress.
- Evaluate the effectiveness of their research strategies.

4. What Types of Problems Do I want Them To Be Able To Solve?
I want them to:

- Know how to do research.
- Solve problems that require geometric proofs.
- Understand the types of problems that trigonometry will help them solve.
- Apply the scientific method.

- Predict consequences.
- Solve problems that have no right answer.
- Make healthy choices.
- Create their own unique expressions.

5. What Concepts and Principles Do I Want My Students to Be Able to Apply?
I want them to be able to:
- Understand what a democracy is.
- Understand cause-and-effect relationships in history and in everyday life.
- Understand the meaning of various logical propositions.
- Criticize literary works based on plot, setting, motive, and so on.
- Understand and recognize the consequences of substance abuse.
- Apply basic principles of ecology and conservation in their everyday lives.

Be as specific as possible in formulating your answers to these questions. While you shouldn't produce the excruciating detail found in behavioral objectives of the past, you should describe your primary outcomes with enough detail that others can agree on what the outcomes mean and whether or not students have attained them.

Using Available Resources

Beyond your own judgments in answering the above questions, you may find it helpful to consult curriculum frameworks, respected content experts, or innovative projects that reflect your educational philosophy. The following are resources you might wish to consider.

National Curriculum Groups

The *Curriculum and Evaluation Standards for School Mathematics*, issued by the National Council of Teachers of Mathematics (1989) is a useful resource. The standards emphasize developing students' capabilities to use mathematics in solving problems, in reasoning, and in communicating. Further, they encourage students to value mathematics and feel self-confident about their ability to do mathematics. For example, the NCTM standards in communication suggest that students be able to:

- Articulate their reasons for using a particular mathematics representation or solution;

- Summarize the meaning of data they have collected;

- Describe how mathematical concepts are related to physical or pictorial models; and

- Justify arguments using deductive or inductive reasoning.

These major goals for student performance may stimulate your thinking about goals you want to set for your students in mathematics.

Actually, many subject discipline groups are developing or have developed goal statements. The American Association for the Advancement of Science (AAAS 1989) makes recommendations for restructuring curriculum in the sciences in *Science for All Americans: Project 2061*. The report recommends four goals for science education: understanding the scientific endeavor, developing scientific views of the world, forming historical and social perspectives on science, and developing scientific habits of mind.

The National Council of Teachers of Social Studies, the National Council of Teachers of Science, and the National Council of Teachers of English are all effective information sources for their disciplines. The Center for Civic Education has published *Civitas*, which covers civic education (Quigley and Bahmueller 1991).

State Curriculum Frameworks

State curriculum frameworks offer another valuable resource. California has led in developing a history-social science framework, including history, geography, economics, political science, anthropology, psychology, sociology, and the humanities (California State Department of Education 1988). The framework includes three major goal areas. Each area contains curriculum strands that spiral up through the course of a student's education:

- Goals of knowledge and cultural understanding
  — historical literacy
  — ethical literacy
  — cultural literacy
  — geographic literacy
  — economic literacy
  — sociopolitical literacy

- Goals of skills attainment and social participation
  — basic study skills
  — critical thinking skills
  — participation skills

- Goals of democratic understanding and civic values
  — national identity
  — Constitutional heritage
  — civic values, rights, and responsibilities

Each of these areas comprises a number of learning goals that could be the subjects of assessment. For example, the participation skills under "goals of skills attainment and social participation" include personal skills, group interaction skills, and social and political participation skills. "Economic literacy" includes specifics related to the basic economic problems facing all societies; comparative economic systems; basic economic goals, performance and societal problems; and the international economic system.

Connecticut has formulated the Common Core of Learning (1987), a set of core learning standards for high school students. The standards include *generic skills* that cross disciplines, and the *big ideas* and *the skills, concepts, processes, and techniques* that characterize a specific discipline. These generic skills provide a starting point for thinking about key student outcomes in any discipline. These generic skills are:

- Communicating clearly;

- Questioning;

- Formulating problems;

- Thinking and reasoning;

- Solving complex, multi-step problems;

- Synthesizing knowledge from a variety of sources; and

- Using cooperation and collaboration.

Connecticut's science skills, processes, and techniques, which are also general, include:

- Developing a hypothesis;

- Designing experiments;

- Drawing inferences from data;

- Using observation and analyzing similarities and differences in phenomena; and

- Working with laboratory equipment.

Other Resources

Frameworks developed for national and international assessments offer another source of information for assessment development. The National Assessment of Educational Progress (NAEP) regularly assesses student performance in mathematics, language arts, science, history, geography, and adult literacy. As part of their process, NAEP conducts a national consensus process that defines the content framework for each assessment and sets priorities for student accomplishment. (For more information, contact the Educational Testing Service, Rosedale Road, Princeton, NJ 08541; telephone (609) 921-9000).

Tapping School Restructuring Efforts

Groups involved in school restructuring efforts offer an additional resource. For example, central to the efforts of the Coalition of Essential Schools is a final exhibition in which students demonstrate their accomplishments. Coalition members have thought carefully about what the nature of those accomplishments should be. Various schools have defined visions of what their graduates should be like at the end of a course or school. Here are just a few examples:

- Students in this course will have a greater understanding of many of the issues that their generation faces. They will speak and write about current events knowledgeably, inquisitively, and honestly. And they will reflect carefully about their roles as presenters of information (Parkway South, contemporary issues).

- Students . . . .most importantly, will know how to apply geometric concepts to real-world situations (Sullivan High School, mathematics).

- Students in this course will know how to work together to produce informative work of high quality. They will have a solid grasp of the field techniques required to study ecology. They will feel proud knowing they have made a tangible contribution to their community . . . .And perhaps most important they will have a strong understanding of and commitment to the natural environment in which they live (Sullivan High School, ecology).

- Graduates of this school will know how to explore ideas in a deep and meaningful way, and they will be able to express their thoughts eloquently, cohesively, and correctly (Sullivan High School, humanities).

- Graduates of Metro High School will have a solid understanding of their interests and talents. They will leave the school confident that they have the skills necessary for their future goals, which they have carefully researched and planned for.

- Graduates of this school will be motivated, insightful, and discriminating adults who think independently and responsibly. They will have considerable knowledge of subject matter, well-developed learning skills . . . (Crefeld School).

Vision statements and descriptions of the exhibitions process are found in *The Exhibitions Collections*, developed and distributed by the Coalition at Brown University. (Contact Joe McDonald, Coalition of Essential Schools, Brown University, Box 1969, Providence, RI 02912; telephone (401) 863-3384; FAX (401) 863-2045.)

Other sources of significant and innovative student outcomes include Henry Levin's Accelerated Learning Project (1989); James Comer's Project (Comer and Haynes-Norris 1991); Elliot Wiggington's Foxfire Project (Puckett 1989); and the Galef Institute's Different Ways of Knowing curriculum (Galef Institute 1992).

Considering Interdisciplinary Goals

Many of the new frameworks being developed show increasing appreciation of interdisciplinary outcomes. The NCTM mathematics standards show attention to communication skills. The AAAS sees math, science, and technology as integrally related and recommends that students understand how powerful ideas of science emerged from particular historical, cultural, and intellectual contexts. The California history-social science framework exemplifies an interdisciplinary curriculum approach as do many of the exhibitions in Coalition Schools. As you proceed with assessment development, you too may want to consider emphasizing interdisciplinary goals for your students.

Consulting with Colleagues

What are the specific targets of your classroom curriculum and your instructional program? In consulting available resources to answer this question, don't neglect your colleagues. Collegial collaboration engenders schoolwide consensus building and better assessments. If you're working on a department, school, or districtwide assessment, you may want to include parents, community members, and representatives from the business sector in the deliberation process.

Setting Meaningful Priorities: A Difficult Proposition

Alone or as part of a group, you'll probably find you've generated a long list of possible targets for performance assessment. As you review your list, either alone or in collaboration with others, you could use the following questions to aid in focusing your assessment:

1. How much **time** will it take students to develop or acquire the skill or accomplishment? If the answer is an hour, a day, or even a week, it's probably not worth the time and effort of a full performance assessment.

2. How does the desired skill or accomplishment **relate to other complex cognitive, social, and affective skills**? Higher priority should be given to skills that are integrally related to other important skills. Give priority to those that will apply to a lot of situations.

3. How does the desired skill or accomplishment **relate to long-term school and curricular goals**? Give priority to the long-term goals, or integral components of important long-term goals.

4. How does the desired skill or accomplishment **relate to your school improvement plan**? Give priority to those that are valued in the plan.

5. What is the **intrinsic importance** of the desired skills or accomplishment? Clearly give priority to those that are important and discard any that represent superficial or trivial goals. (While this seems obvious, think of how many test items you've answered about trivial details.)

6. Are the desired skills and accomplishment **teachable and attainable for your students**? While seeking to challenge students and to draw the highest accomplishment from all students, pay attention to whether or not your students have the necessary prerequisite skills, concepts, and principle knowledge to attain your goals and whether you have the materials and capability to help them reach these goals.

As a result of this type of decision-making process, you will identify what you believe to be a critical set of skills and accomplishments. Each should be described with sufficient specificity so that others understand their meanings. While you may need to revisit and revise these initial descriptions, this priority list will outline the initial targets for the assessment design.

To learn how to develop and conduct alternative assessments, you may want to start with a single assessment. Consider the student outcomes you value most, the time of year, and where you are in the curriculum, and then designate one of your priority outcomes as a first target. Your next job will be to identify appropriate tasks for assessing that target.

References

American Association for the Advancement of Science. (1989). *Project 2061: Science for all Americans.* (Publication No. 89-01S). Washington, D.C.: AAAS.

California State Department of Education. (1988). *History/Social Science Framework for California Public Schools: Kindergarten Through Grade 12.* Sacramento, Calif.: California State Department of Education.

Catterall, J. (1991). *Different Ways of Knowing.* Los Angeles: Galef Institute.

Comer, J., and M. Haynes-Norris (January 1991). "Parent Involvement in Schools: An Ecological Approach." *Elementary School Journal* 91, 3: 271-277.

Connecticut State Board of Education. (January 1987). *Connecticut's Common Core of Learning.* Hartford, Conn.: Connecticut State Department of Education.

Galef Institute. (1992). *Different Ways of Knowing.* (Information packet.) Los Angeles, Galif Institute (11150 Santa Monica Boulevard, Los Angeles, CA 90025).

Levin, H. (May 1989). *Accelerated Schools: A New Strategy for At-risk Students* (Policy Bulletin No. 6). Bloomington, Ind.: Consortium on Educational Policy Studies.

National Council of Teachers of Mathematics. (March 1989). *Curriculum and Evaluation Standards for School Mathematics.* Reston, Va.: NCTM.

Puckett, J.L. (1989). "Who Wrote Foxfire? A Consideration of Ethnohistorical Method." *Journal of Research and Development in Education* 22, 3: 71-78

Quigley, C.N., and C.F. Bahmueller. (1991). *CIVITAS: A Framework for Civic Education.* Calabasas, Calif.: Center for Civic Education.

4

■

Selecting Assessment Tasks

The key to good assessment is matching the assessment task to your intended student outcomes (the knowledge, skills, and dispositions you identified in your initial assessment planning). What tasks or assignments represent these intended accomplishments? You can create many interesting and suitable possibilities. When considering assessment tasks, your best choices are those you believe most closely target your instructional aims and allow your students to demonstrate their progress and capabilities.

As you create interesting tasks for students, you may find that some don't fit your originally designated priorities, but do represent important goals you may have overlooked. This is an example of how the assessment development process is nonlinear. Decisions at each step are influenced by those that precede and follow it. Many teachers find it easier to articulate valued student outcomes *after* thinking about the kinds of student assignments they find most interesting, challenging, and worthwhile.

A number of issues need to be considered in designing appropriate assessment tasks. Figure 4.1 provides a conceptual overview of such issues. Figure 4.1 also clearly portrays the difficulty in thinking about assessment tasks without simultaneously thinking about the criteria you'll use to judge performance on those tasks. While we deal with

Figure 4.1
Assessment Task Map

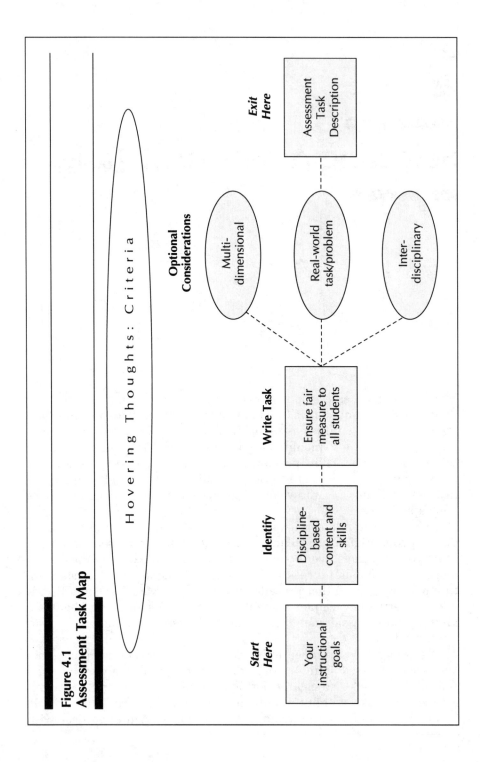

Hovering Thoughts : Criteria

Optional
Considerations

Multi-
dimensional

Real-world
task/problem

Inter-
disciplinary

Exit
Here

Assessment
Task
Description

Write Task

Ensure fair
measure to
all students

Identify

Discipline-
based
content and
skills

Start
Here

Your
instructional
goals

performance criteria in Chapter 5, the separation offers an example that developing assessment is neither simple nor linear.

Choosing Good Tasks

Answering these questions will help you choose effective assessment tasks.

Does the Task Match Specific Instructional Intentions?

When trying to assess a single outcome, it is easy to come up with task ideas. For example, if you want students to communicate effectively in writing, it seems obvious that you should require them to write. But what should they write? If you have not already set specific instructional goals—for instance, the specific kinds of writing you want students to do: narrative, expository, and persuasive—now is the time. Similarly, if you want students to be able to apply the scientific method, having them complete experiments or conduct focused studies seems natural, but you'll also need to decide what specific content and skills the task should involve. What kind of experiments? What kinds of studies: A study of the composition of compost? A community needs survey? A school study of dietary habits? It is important that the assessment task match the specific instructional outcome it is designed to measure.

Does the Task Adequately Represent the Content and Skills You Expect Students to Attain?

According to modern learning theory, content and process are inextricably linked. For example, social studies thinking differs from mathematical thinking. Being able to summarize biology content in writing draws on different knowledge and skills than being able to compose a summary of literature. Therefore, beyond specifying the general nature of the task, you need to think about the specific topics or subject areas you will ask students to address. For example, if you want students to write persuasive pieces, what will provide the basis for their writing? Will it be a hypothetical problem, a school problem, a personal dilemma, a current event, a local issue, a mathematical solution, or an ethical problem? What range of content do you expect them to use—prior knowledge, additional research, or personal knowledge?

Suppose you want students to be able to do science experiments, in particular, chemistry experiments, for problem solving. In deciding on an assessment task, you'll need to consider additional specific content issues. What types of substances should they be able to deal with? What types of problems—analysis, design, or evaluation? And what types of chemical properties and reactions do you want them to incorporate? What types of equipment should they know how to use? In short, what's the range of content, concepts, principles, and techniques with which students should be familiar, and based on these, what's a good example of what you expect of students? Do you want them to analyze unknown substances with particular properties, predict which of several products will work best for a particular purpose, or determine which crop is most cost-efficient for reducing hunger?

Does the Task Enable Students To Demonstrate Their Progress and Capabilities?

Thinking through the specific content you expect in student performance raises several interrelated issues about task fairness and potential bias. What does the task assume about the students' prior knowledge? Have your students had the opportunity to acquire this knowledge? Does the task include skills that are irrelevant to your intended assessment goal? In other word, is the task a fair assessment of what students know and can do and will students be able to show their talents and capabilities? To take another example from writing, we know that students need background knowledge on the topics about which they're expected to write. Without this knowledge, they have nothing to say. Your estimate of students' writing skills is always embedded in what students know (or don't know) about the designated topic. As you formulate specific topics for students, pay attention to the interrelationship between content and skill. Don't hinder students' abilities to demonstrate their skills by throwing something into the assessment that may be irrelevant to your aims. For instance, if your students are not well versed in current events, don't expect them to write an eloquent piece taking a position on a current national issue. Or if your students are not good readers, don't hinder their ability to show their writing skills by having them write about an article you've given them from *The New York Times*. Of course, you have reading goals for students and you may well want them to acquire knowledge about current events, but don't unintentionally confound their ability to show specific skills, or mislabel them as unskilled, based on an inappropriate task or inadequate opportunity to acquire necessary prior knowledge and skills.

One solution to the prior knowledge dilemma is to provide students access to relevant resources, which they know how to use, as part of the assessment situation. For example, high school chemistry students in Connecticut must design and conduct experiments to determine which of two unknown substances is a diet drink and which is a sugared drink. The task assesses different things depending on which textbooks and other resources students are allowed to use. If teachers limit such resources, students' performance will depend on whether they remember specific tests for and the chemical composition of sugars. Students who do not readily recall these facts will not get far in setting up or completing appropriate tests. On the other hand, if teachers allow students access to resources, the task more directly assesses whether students know how to design and conduct scientific experiments, assuming, of course, that their textbooks do not contain the solution for the problem. Which is the better approach? The answer depends on the teacher's intentions and expectations.

Another solution to the prior knowledge dilemma is to provide students a range of options in your assessment task, for instance, by giving them their choice of expression—written, oral, visual, or musical, and a range of tasks of varying difficulty.

Does the Assessment Use Authentic, Real-world Tasks?

Modern curriculum theorists emphasize the importance of engaging students in authentic, real-world tasks because they seem more motivating and have greater transferability than more traditional, decontextualized academic tasks. These theorists also believe that engaging students in the *process* of a discipline as they acquire or demonstrate knowledge in that discipline is a powerful learning strategy. The Connecticut chemistry task, for instance, engages students as scientists and asks them to answer a question they are familiar with in their real world.

Similarly, the Content Assessment Prototype in history, developed by Eva Baker and colleagues (1992) at CRESST, engages students in authentic tasks of historians. Students are asked to read primary source materials, such as an abridged version of the Lincoln-Douglas debates. They must then draw on their prior knowledge and understanding to explain the historical issues addressed by these documents, and incorporate the historical content— the problems and issues facing the nation prior to the Civil War—in their answer. To provide an authentic purpose for the task, the assessment protocol also establishes an appropriate audience for students' responses.

Real-world problems, realistic techniques, and authentic audiences raise innumerable possibilities for tasks. Social studies teachers might have students choose a current problem to research and then write a letter to Congress or the city council, or design a public service advertisement to advocate a solution. Science teachers might have students write letters to their newspapers or state senators, or create a video about ecological problems. Math teachers might have students conduct a survey of community needs and write a report or figure out how much money they'll need to support their future goals, such as buying a car, considering the purchase price, loan/interest costs, insurance, taxes, license, maintenance, gas, and so forth.

Does the Task Lend Itself to an Interdisciplinary Approach?

Authentic, real-world problems don't always conform neatly to separate curriculum domains. Instead, students have to engage knowledge from a variety of disciplines and perspectives. The "letter to the editor about solving an ecological problem" draws on students' communication skills, their science skills in understanding specific ecological problems, and their interpersonal skills in understanding their audience. In another example, a research project task might require a student to research a topic, to design an empirical study based on the scientific facts and principles they research, to use math skills to analyze and display the data from their study, and to apply both their science and communication skills to summarize results and report them to others.

Interdisciplinary tasks offer additional advantages in time and measurement efficiencies. In reality, meaningful performance tasks often take extended periods of time, and there simply may not be enough time to assess all content areas separately. Interdisciplinary tasks help teachers avoid this potential problem.

Can the Task Be Structured To Provide Measures of Several Goals?

It's easy to see that interdisciplinary tasks can be assessed from the perspectives of the separate disciplines involved. For example, because the letter to the editor requires writing skills, interpersonal skills, and science understanding, you can score it separately for performance in each of these areas.

Most assessment tasks designed to measure meaningful goals will also incorporate a range of cognitive, metacognitive, affective, and social skills. For example, the chemistry "soda" task, which takes place over several days, includes these components: group work, individual work, an oral report, and self- and group reflection. In small groups, students must first brainstorm a list of tests that will enable them to determine which of two samples of soda is sugared and which is diet. They then conduct two tests, analyze their results, and present an oral report to the class. Each student is also asked to solve another parallel chemical analysis problem. Students reflect on the strengths and weaknesses of their performances as individuals and as group members, on the performance of other members of the group, and their attitudes toward the task.

Structuring "mega-tasks" to assess a variety of outcomes requires ingenuity. If your high-priority goals include both group and individual work, you might have students work as a group to solve a problem, but work individually during one or more stages of the project, by having each student individually collect and summarize information for a group project. Alternatively, you might want students to work in groups to define and solve a particular problem but have each student present a report of the group's findings. If you want to assess the extent to which students accept challenges and try to solve problems despite the effort and difficulties involved, you would need to leave enough challenge and choice in the assessment task that students can exhibit more or less enthusiasm, effort, and persistence; and include ways for you to observe behavior and affect. Chapter 5 discusses the criteria with which you can judge behavior and affect.

Be aware that while there are advantages and efficiencies in designing such multidimensional, complex, and rich assessment tasks, there are also disadvantages. Chief among these is teasing out from students' responses what is attributable to the skill they've acquired, what is prior knowledge, and even what each student's individual achievement level is. For example, students with limited writing skills will be inhibited from adequately demonstrating their actual level of understanding through writing. Students who are not highly motivated in the face of challenge may quit a long task before they are able to show their level of competence. And if students participate in group work for part of the task, it may be more difficult to judge each individual's achievement.

Generating Good Ideas for Tasks

Brainstorming with colleagues is a good strategy for developing initial ideas for good assessment tasks. You can begin by thinking about the more complex and successful instructional projects you and your colleagues have assigned in the past. Remember the first rule of brainstorming: be creative, write down everything that comes to mind, and don't criticize any ideas until they are all out on the table. Then combine, refine, and embellish the best aspects of each.

Beyond your own ideas, capitalize on the efforts of others. You can adapt and enhance ideas gathered from professional journals, conferences and training sessions, observations of other teachers' classes, and so forth. Be aware that a number of states, school districts, and schools are working to develop these new kinds of assessments. If your state has its own assessment, it may be an idea source. CRESST is assembling a database of efforts across the country and will be distributing them through ERIC. The database will include samples of performance assessments in a variety of subject areas and at a variety of grade levels. While none of these samples will suit your needs and purposes totally, you can borrow the assessment ideas they represent, the scales they use for scoring student performance, and so forth. Even if you are not a chemistry teacher, you may be intrigued by Connecticut's approach to rating group process and may adapt their scales for your own group work. The Lincoln-Douglas/Civil War assessment of understanding and explanation described earlier may provide you with a similar approach in assessing students' social studies, science, or art understanding.

If the assessments you are developing are part of a schoolwide effort, consider involving others in the school community—parents, business representatives, and community members. Those outside the school may be particularly helpful in generating real-world, authentic tasks that exemplify important thinking, problem-solving, and communication skills for students. They can be helpful also as "task reviewers" and in alerting you to the kinds of knowledge, relevant and irrelevant, these tasks represent.

Describing Your Assessment Task

Formal assessment tasks need to be carefully specified or documented so that others can interpret the results or can repeat your methods with other students in other settings. Perhaps even more important, because assessments are supposed to *represent* how a student performs in a larger domain, it is important that *you* know what that broader domain is. A task description helps to describe the larger domain, provides a blueprint for other specific assessments that might be drawn from it, and allows you to review your work and catch major problems before you try them out on students.

While the nature of the assessment task will dictate what needs to be specified, the following aspects usually need specification:

- What outcome(s) are intended for the assessment?

- What are the eligible content/topics?

- What is the nature and format of questions to be posed to students? What is the audience for the response?

- Is it group or individual work? If group work, what roles are to be filled?

- What options/choices are allowed? What are the choices in response mode? What will they include, for example portfolios? Who makes the choices—the teacher or students or both?

- What materials/equipment/resources will be available to students? Are there any specifications?

- What directions will be given to students?

- What administrative constraints are there? How much time is allowed? What is the order of tasks? How will student questions be answered? What help will be allowed?

- What scoring scheme and procedures will be used?

Figure 4.2 on page 42 provides a sample template for your task description. The checklist summarizes both the major concerns associated with creating assessment tasks and the scoring issues to be addressed, which are discussed in the Chapter 5.

Ensuring That Your Tasks Lead
to Sound Assessments

Given the complexity of task development, you will want to review your tasks prior to piloting them with students. These criteria can help you critique your assessment ideas before developing them fully:

- Do the **tasks match the important outcome goals** you have set for students? Do these goals reflect complex thinking skills, such as analysis, and synthesis.

- Do they pose an **enduring** problem type—the types of problems and situations that students are likely to face repeatedly in school and their future lives?

- Are the tasks **fair and free of bias**? For example, do they favor either boys or girls, students who have lived in a particular location or region, students with a particular cultural heritage, or those whose parents can afford to buy certain materials?

- Will the tasks be **credible** to important constituencies? Will they be seen as meaningful and challenging by students, parents, and teachers? Do the tasks rely on quality subject matter content?

- Will the tasks be **meaningful** and engaging to students so that they will be motivated to show their capabilities? Do the tasks involve real problems, situations, and audiences?

Figure 4.2
Checklist for Your Task Description

Outcomes to Be Measured	• Description of instructional goals • Eligible content/Topics • Rules/Process for selection
Assessment Administration Process	• Group/Individual roles • Materials/Equipment • Administration instructions • Help allowed • Time allowed
Actual Question/Problem/ Prompt	• Format • Audience • Options available • Student directions
Scoring	• Rubric/Criteria • Scoring procedures • Use of scores

■ Are the tasks **instructionally related/teachable**? Do they represent skills and knowledge that your students can acquire and that you have the materials and expertise to adequately teach?

■ Are the tasks **feasible** for implementation in your classroom or school in terms of space, equipment, time, costs, and so forth? Are they feasible for students to accomplish in terms of outside of school requirements, including family and other demands on students' time, access to libraries and other resources, and affordability.

These criteria are derived from the more general CRESST criteria for judging assessment quality (Linn et al. 1991). Consideration helps them ensure that assessments yield valid inferences about students and programs.

References

Baker, E.L., P.R. Aschbacher, D. Niemi, and E. Sato. (1992). *CRESST Performance Assessment Models: Assessing Content Area Explanations.* Los Angeles: University of California, Center for Research on Evaluation, Standards and Student Testing.

Linn, R.L., E.L. Baker, and S.B. Dunbar. (1991). "Complex, Performance-based Assessment: Expectations and Validation Criteria." *Education Researcher* 20, 8: 15-23.

5

Setting Criteria

The criteria used for judging student performance lie at the heart of alternative assessment. Although we have discussed selecting and describing assessment tasks separately from developing scoring criteria, these three aspects of assessment are intimately intertwined. In the absence of criteria, assessment tasks remain just that, tasks or instructional activities. Perhaps most important, scoring criteria make public what is being judged and, in many cases, the standards for acceptable performance. Thus, criteria communicate your goals and achievement standards.

Like "alternative assessment" itself, criteria for judging student performance have been called many things, including scoring criteria, scoring guidelines, rubrics, and scoring rubrics. For our purposes, we take all these terms to mean a **description of the dimensions** for judging student performance, a **scale of values** for rating those dimensions, and, when appropriate, the **standards** for judging performance.

Let's take a common example from social studies. You assign students a group presentation accompanied by individual written reports to assess their understanding of history. Because you wish to assess three skills—oral, written, and group process skills as they relate to history—you must consider scoring criteria for each skill. Figure 5.1 on pages

46–47 is a possible set of scoring criteria for just one of these skills, a history group process assessment developed by the California Assessment Program.[1]

The group process exercise taps four **learning outcomes**: group learning, critical thinking, communication, and history knowledge. For each outcome, scoring **dimensions** are specified and levels of performance differentiated by a **scoring scale**. Finally, the scoring guide includes an **evaluation** of each performance level, labeling performance not only in terms of what was accomplished but how well, from minimal to exceptional achievement.

Understanding the Need for Criteria

Criteria are necessary because they help you judge complex human performance in a reliable, fair, and valid manner. Scoring criteria guide your judgments and make public to students, parents, and others the basis for these judgments. Scoring a multiple-choice test does not require complicated judgment; nevertheless, human judgment is still a factor because the test developer phrases the questions and decides what constitutes the best answers. To the person who scores the test, a student either has or has not selected the correct answer; no judgment is needed. When we use selected-response tests, we are essentially corroborating the judgments about adequate performance built into the "answer key." Thus, all assessment, be it selected- or constructed-response, has a subjective or human judgment component.

Alternative assessments invite a wider range of possible responses. Instead of judging responses as right or wrong, alternative assessments judge the quality of, and sometimes the process of, arriving at a complex response. To make such judgments and to ensure their validity, consistency, and fairness, we need criteria or scoring guidelines. Scoring criteria must be well-conceived, explicitly defined, and consistently applied. Well-specified criteria help to ensure that everyone understands what is expected.

Well-articulated and publicly visible criteria for judging student responses are necessary and useful whether the results will be used in

---

[1]Many of the examples we use throughout this book are from state assessment programs, especially those in California. Because of their pioneering work in developing curriculum frameworks reflecting current learning and curriculum theory, certain states have already field-tested promising prototypes for alternative assessment that can be adapted for classroom use.

Figure 5.1
California Assessment Program 1990
History-Social Science Grade 11
Scoring Guide: Group Performance Task

	Level I Minimal Achievement	Level II Rudimentary Achievement	Level III Commendable Achievement	Level IV Superior Achievement	Level V Exceptional Achievement
Group and Collaborative Learning 20	(1-4) Exclusive reliance on one spokesperson. Little interaction. Very brief conversations. Some students are disinterested or distracted.	(5-9) Strong reliance on spokespersons. Only one or two persons actively participate. Sporadic interaction. Conversation not entirely centered on topic.	(8-12) Some ability to interact. At least half the students confer or present ideas. Attentive reading of documents and listening. Some evidence of discussion of alternatives.	(13-16) Students show adeptness in interacting. At least 3/4 of students actively participate. Lively discussion centers on the task.	(17-20) Almost all students enthusiastically participate. Responsibility for task is shared. Students reflect awareness of others' views and opinions and include references to other opinions or alternatives in presentation and answer. Questions and answers illustrate forethought and preparation.
Critical Thinking 30	(1-6) Demonstrates little understanding and only limited comprehension of scope of problem or issues. Employs only the most basic parts of information provided. Mixes fact and opinion in developing a viewpoint. States conclusion after hasty or cursory look at only one or two pieces of information. Does not consider consequences.	(7-12) Demonstrates only a very general understanding of scope of problem. Focuses on a single issue. Employs only the information provided. May include opinion as well as fact in developing a position. States conclusion after limited examination of evidence with little concern for consequences.	(13-18) Demonstrates a general understanding of scope of problem and more than one of the issues involved. Employs the main points of information from the documents and at least one general idea from personal knowledge to develop a position. Builds conclusion on examination of information and some consideration of consequences.	(19-24) Demonstrates clear understanding of scope of problem and at least two central issues. Uses the main points of information from the documents and personal knowledge that is relevant and consistent in developing a position. Builds conclusion on examination of the major evidence. Considers at least one alternative action and the possible consequences.	(25-30) Demonstrates a clear, accurate understanding of the scope of the problem and the ramifications of the issues involved. Employs all information from the documents and extensive personal knowledge that is factually relevant, accurate, and consistent in the development of a position. Bases conclusion on a thorough examination of the evidence, an exploration of reasonable alternatives, and an evaluation of consequences.

Figure 5.1 (continued)

	Level I Minimal Achievement	Level II Rudimentary Achievement	Level III Commendable Achievement	Level IV Superior Achievement	Level V Exceptional Achievement
Communi-cation of Ideas 20	(1-4) Position is vague. Presentation is brief and includes unrelated general statements. Overall view of the problem is not clear. Statements tend to wander or ramble.	(5-9) Presents general and indefinite position. Only minimal organization in presentation. Uses generalities to support position. Emphasizes only one issue. Considers only one aspect of problem.	(8-12) Takes a definite but general position. Presents a somewhat organized argument. Uses general terms with limited evidence that may not be totally accurate. Deals with a limited number of issues. Views problem within a somewhat limited range.	(13-16) Takes a clear position. Presents an organized argument with perhaps only minor errors in the supporting evidence. Deals with the major issues and shows some understanding of relationships. Gives consideration to examina-tion of more than one idea or aspect of the problem.	(17-20) Takes a strong, well-defined position. Presents a well-organized, persuasive argument with accurate supporting evidence. Deals with all significant issues and demonstrates a depth of understanding of important relationships. Examines the problem from several positions.
Knowledge and Use of History 30	(1-6) Reiterates one or two facts without complete accuracy. Deals only briefly and vaguely with concepts or the issues. Barely indicates any previous historical knowledge. Relies heavily on the information provided.	(7-12) Provides only basic facts with only some degree of accuracy. Refers to information to explain at least one issue or concept in general terms. Limited use of previous historical knowledge without complete accuracy. Major reliance on the information provided.	(13-18) Relates only major facts to the basic issues with a fair degree of accuracy. Analyzes information to explain at least one issue or concept with substantive support. Uses general ideas from previous historical knowledge with fair degree of accuracy.	(19-24) Offers accurate analysis of the documents. Provides facts to relate to the major issues involved. Uses previous general historical knowledge to examine issues involved.	(25-30) Offers accurate analysis of the information and issues. Provides a variety of facts to explore major and minor issues and concepts involved. Extensively uses previous historical knowledge to provide an in-depth understanding of the problem and to relate it to past and possible future situations.

the classroom or to make school level or national decisions. In all assessment settings, scoring criteria must:

- Help teachers define excellence and plan how to help students achieve it.
- Communicate to students what constitutes excellence and how to evaluate their own work.
- Communicate goals and results to parents and others.
- Help teachers or other raters be accurate, unbiased, and consistent in scoring.
- Document the procedures used in making important judgments about students.

Criteria and Instructional Planning

Scoring criteria clarify instructional goals. Along with the task description, the criteria define priority outcomes in terms of the content to be covered, the knowledge or skills to be demonstrated, and the context in which these are to occur. The complete alternative assessment specifications can guide selection and sequencing of relevant instructional activities.

Criteria and Students

The criteria for alternative assessments are often made public and are intended to be discussed with students. Public discussions help students to internalize the standards and "rules" they need to become independent learners. Alternative assessments and their criteria can be woven into the fabric of the curriculum so that they are transparent to the student and perceived as a natural part of the learning process. Such assessment is ongoing and takes many forms—journals, conferences, peer or teacher coaching episodes, critiques of products and exhibitions, and formal evaluations of individual works or a body of work. Examples of what constitutes good work engage students in the work itself and in judgments about their work. Public discussions of quality and criteria inform students during the formative period of instruction, not simply at the end of a unit or course when it is too late to make improvements. Furthermore, discussions of criteria also help students see the perspectives of their teachers, their peers, and sometimes even the experts in the field.

Criteria and Parent Involvement

Clearly articulated criteria also communicate to parents and others what the teachers and schools are trying to accomplish. Criteria operationalize learning goals and expectations for children. When parents know prior to grading what is expected, they can support their child's learning. For example, giving parents of kindergartners a copy of "Profile of Developmental Outcomes for Kindergarten" (Figure 5.2) allows them to work with their children at home on activities such as recognizing beginning letters or sight words. The road to literacy is well-marked; teachers who share the map with parents may find that more of their students reach their destinations in a timely manner.

Good criteria help both students and parents share some of the responsibility for learning. Parents and children who are familiar with the standards by which work is judged are less likely to ascribe poor performance to such external factors as not being told what was important or personality conflicts between teachers and students.

Criteria and Consistency

When guidelines for what constitutes good work are vague or unstated, it is difficult to be consistent, fair, and accurate in judging student responses. With selected-response tests, accuracy and consistency in scoring refers to whether the test score for an individual pupil remains fairly stable from one testing occasion to another, in the absence of intervening instruction or growth. This consistency is better known as reliability. For alternative assessments, reliability includes not only the idea of the stability of an individual student's performance over time but also the stability of a rater's judgments of that performance. Specifically, a reliable assessment that depends on human judgment must meet the following requirements:

- Several judges looking at a specific task would come to the same conclusion about a student.
- Each judge would rate the student's performance on a specific task about the same on a subsequent occasion.
- The student would perform the same task at about the same level on different occasions.
- If the task is meant to represent or generalize to some larger domain, the sample is representative of that domain.

Figure 5.2
Profile of Developmental Outcomes for Kindergarten Literacy and Numeracy Skills

Joan C. Hillard, Superintendent, Spreckels Union School District, Spreckels, California
Elizabeth Jones, Professor, Pacific Oaks College, Pasadena, California
Jane Meade-Roberts, Director and Owner, Power of Play Preschool, Salinas, California
San Vincente School, Soledad Union School District, Soledad, California
(Jones and Meade-Roberts 1990)

Oral language	Is nonverbal in school	Uses language to satisfy basic wants and needs	Often uses language in play and conversation with peers	Clearly describes real or imaginary situations using complex descriptive language	Speaks in whole sentences using a well-developed vocabulary
Drawing	Scribbles	Draws a face	Adds arms/legs	Adds body with arms/legs	Adds details (hair, ear, hands, etc.)
Writing	Scribbles and pretends to write	Uses letters or letter like signs to represent writing	Spontaneously writes own name including all letters	Spontaneously copies words	Can invent spelling of words using phonetic clues
Reading	Reads own name	Recognizes beginning letter of first name when written in other places	Recognizes own name, other letters and numerals	Recognizes and reads sight words, including signs, labels, key words, teacher-created word lists and/or words in books	Uses knowledge of letter sounds to sound out words

50

Figure 5.2 (continued)

Attitudes toward literacy	Not yet interested in books or writing	Demonstrates focused interest in picture books	Demonstrates interest in written language (e.g., asks about or reads signs, names, words in class, labels, words in books)	Spontaneously practices writing letters and numerals	Demonstrates interest in writing correctly
Problem solving using classification	Randomly manipulates objects	Spontaneously orders by likenesses and differences	Recognizes or creates simple (AB) patterns using a variety of materials and/or symbols	Recognizes or creates complex (e.g., AABAAB) patterns using a variety of materials and/or symbols	Can classify by more than one attribute at a time (e.g., size and color)
Problem solving using numbers	Calls numerals at random	Counts by rote	Demonstrates understanding of one to one correspondence (e.g., evaluates objects accurately)	Is able to use knowledge of counting to solve real problems	Demonstrates conservation of number (e.g., understands that number of objects remains constant)

Figure 5.2 (continued)

Curiosity	Watches silently	Asks cautious questions	Asks questions constantly	Asks questions appropriately	Uses resources to find answers to questions (e.g., experimenting, taking risks, solving problems)
Creativity	Waits to be told what to do	Explores available materials	Invents a simple dramatization or projects with provided materials	Asks or looks for not already available materials to accomplish project/play idea	Works competently on notably complex, creative, imaginative, self-initiated tasks
Social skills with peers	Usually observes play with others	Usually plays alone or is involved in parallel play	Is developing cooperative play skills	Socially self-confident; plays effectively with other children	Has well-developed skills of leadership and cooperation in play
Social skills with adults/groups	Accepts situations rather than ask for adult help	Communicates with adults primarily to get help	Speaks spontaneously and freely with adults	Participates in group activities and conversation	Is sensitive to and articulate about the needs of others

Figure 5.2 (continued)

Large motor skills	Runs	Jumps	Hops on one foot	Catches a ball with arms and chest	Can catch ball with hands only
Fine motor skills	Scribbles with crayon/pencil	Able to use scissors	Colors inside lines/cuts on lines	Draws/writes accurate lines	Consistently neat work
New learning	Chooses to observe	Prefers familiar tasks	Willing to try new tasks	Masters new tasks quickly	Masters new tasks independently
Social knowledge	Knows colors	Knows shapes	Knows personal information	Knows names of letters and numbers	Knows days of week, months
Attention span	Rapidly changing	Focuses on self-selected tasks	Focus on teacher-selected tasks	Works independently on self- and teacher-selected tasks	Can follow complex directions and maintain focused attention for long periods

(From E. Jones and J.M. Roberts, *Profile of Developmental Outcomes for Kindergarten, Literacy and Numeracy Skills*, San Vicente School, Soledad CA)

It is easy to see how these four requirements for reliable scoring demand a mechanism for creating rater agreement and for delineating clearly the domains of particular assessment tasks. Scoring criteria must meet this demand.

Criteria and Consequences

Specifying criteria is always important and becomes even more so when the consequences of an assessment are very serious, such as when results are used for retention, graduation, or placement in special programs. Clear guidelines for evaluating student work ensure appropriate consequences for students and the educational system as a whole. Furthermore, when alternative assessments are used for these high-stakes decisions, the scoring procedures and criteria must be legally defensible and adhere to the due process standards of a court of law.

Specifying Criteria

Different testing purposes require different kinds of scoring criteria. Many of the examples in this book were developed for state-level assessments with such high-stakes testing purposes as comparing schools, identifying low-performing schools, and evaluating individual schools. The California Assessment Program (CAP) history group process criteria (shown in Figure 5.1.) are an example of the complex criteria used in high-stakes assessment. Because the criteria are used for a one-shot state assessment, the scoring guide was developed to extract the maximum amount of information possible during limited assessment time. We see that the criteria:

- List multiple learning outcomes.
- Divide each outcome into performance levels.
- Describe traits/characteristics for each level.
- Provide a numerical scale to rate the degree to which each level was attained.
- Evaluate the quality of student performance represented by the different levels using such descriptors as "minimal achievement" or "excellent achievement."

Your criteria will be less complex when your testing purposes are more focused and the decisions you wish to make about students are limited.

If you are using student academic journals to monitor their progress in making connections between science lessons and their daily lives, your scoring criteria may be to count the number of unprompted statements connecting classroom learning with out-of-class experiences. The number of connections you find will tell you whether you are achieving your goals. Your assessment purpose here may be formative—to improve your instruction and to identify students who need more help or a different approach.

Perhaps your assessment purpose is more traditional—you want to evaluate student progress toward meeting your goals in mathematics problem solving. Your scoring criteria might resemble the generalized rubric for essay-type mathematics problems developed by the CAP (shown in Figure 5.3). The criteria provide descriptions of each level of performance in terms of what students are able to do, assign values to these levels, then apply standards at certain cut points. Students rated 1-2 are evaluated as having "inadequate" responses; students rated 3-4 receive a "satisfactory"; and students receiving 5-6 are rated "competent."

While grading is a complex issue and the scores of any one alternative assessment may or may not be used to assign grades, it is possible to find or develop criteria linked specifically to letter grades. Researchers funded by the National Science Foundation have developed a grade-linked set of criteria to assess student's procedural knowledge in a hands-on science experiment (Baxter et al. 1992). The researchers determined which methods students could use to solve the problem posed by the experiment, judged which would produce the most logical and efficient solutions, then created grade-referenced criteria to reflect their evaluations of the solutions. A summary of how their criteria is linked to grades appears in Figure 5.4.

Regardless of the testing purpose, the sample criteria have four common elements. Each has

- One or more traits or **dimensions** that serve as the basis for judging the student response
- **Definitions and examples** to clarify the meaning of each trait or dimension
- A **scale** of values (or a counting system) on which to rate each dimension
- **Standards** of excellence for specified performance levels accompanied by models or examples of each level.

Figure 5.3
CAP Generalized Rubric
(California State Department of Education 1989)

Demonstrated Competence

Exemplary Response . . . Rating = 6
Gives a complete response with a clear, coherent, unambiguous, and elegant explanation; includes a clear and simplified diagram; communicates effectively to the identified audience; shows understanding of the open-ended problem's mathematical ideas and processes; identifies all the important elements of the problem; may include examples and counterexamples; presents strong supporting arguments.

Competent Response . . . Rating = 5
Gives a fairly complete response with reasonably clear explanations; may include an appropriate diagram; communicates effectively to the identified audience; shows understanding of the problem's mathematical ideas and processes; identifies the most important elements of the problems; presents solid supporting arguments.

Satisfactory Response

Minor Flaws But Satisfactory . . . Rating = 4
Completes the problem satisfactorily, but the explanation may be muddled; argumentation may be incomplete; diagram may be inappropriate or unclear; understands the underlying mathematical ideas; uses mathematical ideas effectively.

Serious Flaws But Nearly Satisfactory . . . Rating = 3
Begins the problem appropriately but may fail to complete or may omit significant parts of the problem; may fail to show full understanding of mathematical ideas and processes; may make major computational errors; may misuse or fail to use mathematical terms; response may reflect an inappropriate strategy for solving the problem.

Inadequate Response

Begins, But Fails to Complete Problem . . . Rating = 2
Explanation is not understandable; diagram may be unclear; shows no understanding of the problem situation; may make major computational errors.

Unable to Begin Effectively . . . Rating = 1
Words do not reflect the problem; drawings misrepresent the problem situation; copies parts of the problem but without attempting a solution; fails to indicate which information is appropriate to problem.

No Attempt . . . Rating = 0

Figure 5.4
Linking Criteria to Grades

Grade	Criteria for Determining Grades
A	Student selects method. Student saturates towels. Student determines result so as to answer question. Result logically follows from method used to saturate towel. Measurements are accurate/carefully done. Conclusions are correct.
B	Meets all requirements of an "A" but measurement is careless.
C	Meets all requirements of "A" but may be deficient in some areas. Must attempt to control saturation by putting the same amount of water on each towel. Towels not saturated (key dimension for determining a "C" or below grade).
D	Student fails to saturate towels or control for saturation. Result is logically inconsistent with method used to saturate towels.
F	Student did not conduct the investigation Or, equipment manipulated without purpose Or, towels not wet Or, conclusions based on how towels felt.

*Criteria abridged from Baxter et al. (1992, p. 5).

Considerations in Selecting Dimensions

The dimensions you use to assess student performance in a certain domain should reflect the essential qualities of good performance in that domain. Where do you find these essential qualities? The qualities or dimensions can be provided by non-educator experts, colleagues in your department, grade level teachers, district curriculum committees, research literature, and national, state, or local subject area standards committees. If you are creating criteria for your own classroom, focus your criteria on those aspects of student performance that reflect your highest priority instructional goals and represent teachable and observable aspects of performance.

One way to uncover dimensions for scoring criteria is to ask yourself the following kinds of questions:

- What are the attributes of good writing, of good scientific thinking, of good collaborative group process, of effective oral presentation? More generally, by what qualities or features will I know whether students have produced an excellent response to my assessment task?

- How does completing this task relate to my goals for students? What will they do that shows me we are working towards or achieving some of these goals?

- What do I expect to see if this task is done excellently, acceptably, poorly?

- Do I have samples or models of student work, from my class or other sources, that exemplify some of the criteria I might use in judging this task?

- What criteria for this or similar tasks exist in my state curriculum frameworks, my state assessment program, my district curriculum guides, my school assessment program?

- What dimensions might I adapt from work done by national curriculum councils, by other teachers?

In addition to describing your judgments about performance, the dimensions you use for your criteria need to be written so that all audiences who use them will understand them in the same way. Perhaps you are judging an interdisciplinary art project designed to reflect social studies understanding of the relationship of Native Americans to their environment. Your criteria for assigning grades or judging levels of performance should be clear to students, parents, and other teachers who depend on your judgments about content mastery, be they others at your grade level or those teaching your students next year.

Clear descriptions of performance dimensions can be achieved in several ways:

1. You could write definitions in terms of the behaviors or elements you will see when judging students. For example, instead of saying, "Acceptable performance means students show an understanding of living in harmony with the land," you could say, "Acceptable performance means that student drawings depict an environment that is almost unchanged from its original state. Few trees are cut; grassland is undisturbed except for small sustenance patches; no large waste dumps exist, and so on."

2. You could provide models or examples for each dimension. This

is commonly done in direct writing assessments. Teachers are given copies of student essays exemplifying each point in the score distribution. The essays illustrate such dimensions as, "the essay is well organized; it begins and ends effectively." From these, teachers and others can articulate precise definitions of each dimension.

3. If you are assessing informally, you could clarify your dimensions as a set of questions. For example, when you are assessing journals to see what kinds of help students need in developing fluency in writing, your criteria for deciding what to work on next could include the following questions: Which students are using some pre-writing strategies such as clustering, drawing, listing, or free-writing? Which students are keeping a log of writing ideas? Which students are having spelling problems that block the flow of ideas?

Unambiguous scale definitions usually consist of a description of the dimension to be rated, plus examples of student work illustrating acceptable responses. These models or work samples are crucial in developing a consensus about the meaning of criteria when used for rater training in formal assessments. Models also provide students with concrete examples of what acceptable or excellent work can look like. Figure 5.5 details one of several dimensions in a scoring rubric developed by CRESST to assess the depth of high school students' understanding of history as revealed in their essays. Note that dimensions and scale points are thoroughly operationalized: key terms, such as "concept," are defined and examples of basic points, such as statements of opinion, are provided.

In most cases, your performance dimensions, particularly for classroom assessment, will reflect your views of what constitutes excellence or expertise and will be moderated by your expectations for students at different grade levels and by your instructional goals at different points in the school year. Because your criteria help students focus on what's important instructionally, you may use different criteria at different times during the school year. For example, while you may feel that organization and mechanics are an important part of expressing discipline-based knowledge in history or science, at the beginning of the year you may particularly want to encourage fluency. Thus, your criteria at the beginning of the semester will stress the number of ideas presented, number of examples or definitions for each idea, and so on. As students become more fluent and able to substantiate their views, you can expand your criteria to include organization and mechanics. To take an example from figure skating, you may believe in the Olympic criteria of "technical

Figure 5.5
CRESST Content Area Explanation Essay Scoring Guidelines
(Baker, Aschbacher, Niemi, and Sato 1992)

CRESST Scoring Rubric Scales:
General Impression—Content Quality
Number of Principles or Concepts
Prior Knowledge: Facts and Events
Argumentation
Misconceptions
Text details

Example of Guidelines for the *Number of Principles or Concepts* Scale:

Number of Principles/Concepts

This is a measure of the number of different social studies concepts or principles that the student uses with comprehension.

A *concept* is an abstract, general notion, such as "inflation." It does not refer to particular events or objects (such as one particular period of inflation), but instead represents features common to a category of events or objects. "Imperialism," for example, does not refer to any specific facts or events; it is a heading that characterizes a class of behaviors and beliefs. "Industrialization" likewise identifies a class of activities and events that share common properties. It must be clear that the student is using a term conceptually, not just as a label.

A *principle* is a rule or belief used to justify an action or judgment, as in the statement "Slavery is immoral," where "morality" serves as a justifying principle.

It should be evident that the student understands the concept and means to discuss it. The concept should not simply be mentioned within a quotation from the text with no indication that the student grasps the concept. To earn a score point, the concept or principle need not be named explicitly, such as, "Constitutionality was an important principle that influenced the debate over slavery," but the idea should be stated clearly, for example, "One problem was determining what the constitution said about slavery."

Score point guidelines:
0—no response
1—no concepts/principles
2—one concept/principle
3—two concepts/principles
4—three concepts/principles
5—four or more concepts/principles

Example: "One great factor that held us back from war was our economy. It was not known what would happen to our economy without the safety of Britain. Britain could defend our commerce and coasts. Also, with Britain there was a great advantage with exportation. It seemed our economy could only suffer without the aid of Britain."

merit" and "artistic expression" but at different points in your teaching you may want to differentially emphasize one or the other.

Dimensions for Complex Tasks

As we mention in Chapter 4, it is entirely possible to create a complex assessment with multiple intended outcomes. Multiple outcomes require multiple criteria, a set for each outcome. Multidimensional criteria are unavoidable when you are doing interdisciplinary assessment or judging complex learning goals. You may either formulate separate criteria for each of these outcomes or create a multidimensional set of criteria. Connecticut's state assessment in science incorporates two approaches to assessing the same task by providing criteria for assessing group process and individual accomplishment (see Figures 5.6 and 5.7). Another perspective on student performance is provided by the subskills within the individual and group assessments. When examining group process skills, we are interested in scientific process, communication, and group collaboration. Separate criteria attend to each of these skills. The multiple dimensions on the individual scale include content and communication outcomes.

The dimensions for each scale require a lot of inference. Both teachers and students would need further descriptions of such dimensions as "draw reasonable conclusions" or "collaborate effectively" in order to use the scales. In fact, these scales are used in classrooms only after teachers have had inservice training to discuss the meaning of the dimensions, review examples, and practice using the criteria. Through classroom discussion and examples students and teachers come to a mutual understanding of the dimensions of the individual scale.

A less complex example of multidimensional criteria appears in Figure 5.1. The criteria assess four group performance outcomes: collaboration, critical thinking, communication, and history knowledge. The criteria include sub-criteria for deciding at which of five performance levels we should place students for each outcome. The entire set of group process criteria may be viewed as a compendium of four sets of criteria, one for collaboration, one for critical thinking, one for communication, and one for history knowledge.

Using Rating Scales

All sample scoring criteria included in this chapter contain some type of scale, either numerical, qualitative, or both. The criteria in Figure 5.1,

Figure 5.6
PART II: Objectives Rating Form — Group

Title of the Task: _____ Task # _____

Teacher ID #: _____ Date: _____

Student I.D. #'s
1. _____
2. _____
3. _____
4. _____
5. _____

The group should be able to…	Where to Find Evidence					E	G	N.I.	*
	Group Report (Page #)	Oral Presentation	Teacher Observation	Other (Specify)					
1. Identify and apply physical and/or chemical properties for the purpose of identification.						○	○	○	
2. Formulate predictions based on prior knowledge.						○	○	○	
3. Identify information and steps needed to solve a problem.						○	○	○	
4. Test predictions.						○	○	○	
5. Gather data pertinent to a problem.						○	○	○	
6. Make inferences based on pertinent data.						○	○	○	
7. Draw reasonable conclusions and defend them rationally.						○	○	○	
8. Communicate the strategies and outcomes of a study through written means.						○	○	○	
9. Orally communicate the strategies and outcomes of a study.						○	○	○	
10. Collaborate effectively.						○	○	○	
* Check if students' work is a strong and clear example of rating given.						○	○	○	

(Connecticut Department of Education 1990)   E = Excellent   G = Good   N.I. = Needs Improvement

Figure 5.7
PART II: Objectives Rating Form — Individual

Title of the Task: _____ Task # _____ Student ID # _____

Teacher ID #: _____ Date: _____

The group should be able to...	Where to Find Evidence				E	G	N.I.	*
1. Identify and apply physical and/or chemical properties for the purpose of identification.					○	○	○	
2. Identify information and steps needed to solve a problem.					○	○	○	
3. Communicate the strategies of a study through written means.					○	○	○	
					○	○	○	
					○	○	○	
					○	○	○	
					○	○	○	
					○	○	○	
					○	○	○	

* Check if students' work is a strong and clear example of rating given.

(Connecticut Department of Education 1990) E = Excellent G = Good N.I. = Needs Improvement the history group process, and Figure 5.3, the mathematics problem, contain both numerical and qualitative rating scales. Figure 5.4, the hands-on science criteria, and Figures 5.6 and 5.7, the group and individual science experiment, have qualitative ratings only, such as letter grades or evaluations such as "excellent" or "needs improvement."

Why scales? How do you know whether to use numerical or qualitative ratings? What about using a checklist instead of a rating scale? Whether you rate the presence or absence of a performance, as in a checklist, or use numbers or qualitative evaluations will depend on your testing purpose. There are three major types of scales: checklists, numerical ratings, and qualitative (either descriptive or evaluative) ratings. If your purpose is to **describe** what students can do, perhaps for parent conferences or to compare student performance to certain developmental standards, you may be able to use the simplest rating scale of all, the checklist. If you need more information than simply whether or not a student is engaged in specific aspects of a task, you will need a more fully developed rating scale. When you want to know the **extent** to which dimensions were observed or the **quality** of the performance, you need more elaborate scales. Rating scales, beyond the yes-no checklist format, reflect aspects of student performance other than mere accomplishment of an activity.

Checklists

A checklist is a list of dimensions, characteristics, or behaviors that are essentially scored as "yes-no" ratings. A check indicates that either the characteristic or behavior was present or absent. Checklists often contain more dimensions to be scored than do rating scales, but those dimensions are often quite narrow and concrete.

Checklists can be useful in assessing processes, an important purpose for teachers concerned with the how as well as the what of learning. A process checklist for a hands-on experiment could resemble Figure 5.8, which asks the rater to note the presence of specified behaviors.

Primary school teachers find checklists useful because they must often determine how students are developing according to some theory of skills acquisition. For example, current language acquisition theory suggests that this skill cluster supports a child's ability to read:

- Ability to draw or depict an idea
- Ability to recognize sound-letter correspondence
- Ability to recognize that words stand for something

- Knowledge of left to right and up-to-down page orientation
- Ability to recall and retell favorite stories

Figure 5.8
Process Checklist

Procedure	Check if Observed	Comments
Selected approach		
Correct equipment used		
Measurement accurate		
Sought peer help if needed		
Recorded observations		
Cleaned up after experiment		

The teacher can document acquisition of these readiness skills with a checklist. There is no need to judge how well each of these behaviors are displayed, only that they are in place. Figure 5.2 demonstrates a developmentally-based profile for kindergartners created by teachers of the Soledad Union School District in California, with consultation from Pacific Oaks College in Pasadena, California. This is an example of a theory-based profile. The profile development process was designed to help staff better understand constructivism, the developmental learning theory on which it is based. The behaviors identified in Figure 5.2 are sequenced from left to right in the order that the kindergarten staff predicted that those behaviors are acquired. This document was designed to be re-analyzed each year as teachers observe children's behaviors from a developmental point of view.

Numerical Scales

A numerical scale uses numbers or assigns points to a continuum of performance levels. The length of the continuum or the number of scale points can vary, three points, four points, five points, seven points—any number is possible. How many divisions or scale points should a good scale include? While there's no single answer to this question, our experience suggests that you consider these issues.

The number of points or divisions on a scale can and should vary depending on what decisions you will be making about students and whether the scale will be used in the classroom or in a formal scoring session with several raters involved in judging performance. In general, the larger the scale, the more difficult it is to clearly differentiate among the score points. Consider how quickly you can sort essays into stacks worthy of zero points, one point, or two points; essentially a decision among low, medium, and high. Why use a ten-point scale if you really only want to distinguish two or three groups of students, such as those who need additional instruction on writing a well-organized essay and those who don't?

A scale with only a few points does have some disadvantages. More scale points enable you to identify small differences between individual students and may provide more diagnostic information than a reduced scale. For example, a longer scale may be needed if you want to use one scale for all students K–12 and you also want to differentiate among students in a single grade. Also, if your scale will be used for formal assessment purposes where several readers will be rating each performance, any statistics you have to calculate, such as rater agreement, will be affected by the scale range. Using a shorter scale will result in a high percent agreement, but it will be more difficult to achieve a high correlation between raters' scores (two different ways of figuring inter-rater reliability).

It takes longer to arrive at consensus about how to assign scale points when there are more points to consider. With a five- or six-point scale, raters often refer to prior experience and assign the lowest points to off-task or truly terrible performances, the highest to stellar examples, reserve the middle for "passing," "acceptable," or model performances, then allocate those not fitting into the three anchor points to the remaining scale values. An eleven- or seventeen-point scale makes it more difficult for raters to anchor their judgments in prior experience. However, you will often see scales in multiples of five, such as ten, fifteen, or twenty point scales, which allow readers to "chunk" the points into five-point intervals. Initial rating distinctions are then really made between a five and a ten rather than a four and a seven with examples not clearly fitting into the increments receiving the intermediate points.

Another consideration related to scale size concerns multidimensional criteria. If you are rating the same performance with several criteria, each assessing a different outcome, you may want to use the same number of scale points for each outcome. Not only does this make it possible to aggregate or compare the results of several scales, but it eases the rating task. For example, using a four-point scale for coherence and a five-point scale for supporting facts could slow the rating process while raters mentally shift to different scale points. Students trying to understand their relative strengths and weaknesses can also have difficulty comparing different scales. However, if you want some outcomes to count more than others for a total score, you can use different size scales to reflect relative value or weight. A good example of this strategy appears in Figure 5.1, the history group process task. The scoring guide uses two different scales with one set of outcomes "weighted" up to twenty points and the other up to thirty.

Qualitative Scales

A qualitative scale uses adjectives rather than numbers to characterize student performance. These scales are of two general sorts, descriptive and evaluative. Descriptive scales label student performance but don't necessarily make explicit the standards underlying the judgment; they use fairly neutral terms to characterize performance. Judgments about task completion, task understanding, or the appearance of certain elements in the performance are typical descriptors. Figure 5.9 provides three examples of descriptive scales that do not evaluate the worth of student performance.

Figure 5.9
Descriptive Scales

No evidence...Minimal evidence...Partial evidence...Complete evidence.

Task not attempted...Partial completion...Completed...Goes beyond.

Off task...Attempts to address task...Minimal attention to task...Addresses task but no elaboration...Fully elaborated and attentive to task and audience.

Evaluative scales incorporate judgments of worth anchored in underlying standards of excellence. The most commonly used evaluative scales are grades (see Figure 5.4). Scales using descriptors of "excellence" (Figures 5.1, 5.6, and 5.7) or judging competence (Figure 5.3) are evaluative in nature. Evaluative scales require higher levels of inference to interpret than descriptive scales. The inferences are made by referring directly to the scoring criteria. The criteria themselves embed notions of excellence, competence, or acceptable outcomes.

Numerical-Qualitative Scales

Numerical scales are often easier for people to remember, to aggregate, and to average, but are difficult to interpret in the absence of good descriptors. After all, a score of "4" on a six-point scale may connote different levels or qualities of attainment to different people. Good criteria often include both descriptive and numerical values. For example, Figure 5.3 displays a draft of a scale used by the California Assessment Program for judging open-ended math problems. Note that it is both numeric and descriptive. Performance is rated numerically, but each numerical score is attached to an evaluation ranging from "inadequate" to "competent."

Whether your scale values are numerical, descriptive, or both, it is important to make sure that scales help parents, students, teachers, administrators, and policymakers understand the meaning of the performance in the same way. This common understanding helps ensure reliable and fair judgments.

The Link with Standards

Nearly all criteria, even descriptive checklists, are linked in some way to standards—the expectations for student performance. Grades or qualitative ratings reflect teacher judgment, or in the case of the hands-on science criteria in Figure 5.4, the consensus of the rating team. The standards underlying different scales may reflect either criterion-referenced or norm-referenced approaches to judging quality. The mathematics criteria (Figure 5.3) with descriptors for "inadequate response," "satisfactory response," and "demonstrated competence," reflect an absolute standard or mastery approach to standard setting. The descriptors clearly indicate good or desired performance levels, "satisfactory and above," versus poor levels, "inadequate." The levels are referenced to discipline-based standards, mathematics teachers' conceptions of adequate problem-solving strategies.

Another example is Illinois' six-point writing assessment scale, which employs an absolute scale and is designed to be used across grade levels. A score of six represents an extremely high level of writing, and few if any elementary students are expected to score above a "3." This type of scale is especially useful in measuring growth over years. The limitation of an absolute scale for multigrade/age assessment is that because elementary students all tend to score near the bottom of the scale, there is little variability in their scores so it is impossible to tell much about them individually from their scores. They all "look alike."

Other evaluative scales reflect norm-referenced approaches to standard setting. When grades or points are assigned by comparing students' relative status, such as, 'Maria's essay was better than the class average',", "Gary's video was among the best in the class," the standards are norm-referenced. Developmental checklists or scales demonstrate another common use of norm-referenced scales in alternative assessment. The sequencing of behaviors in these scales rests on what educators and others have observed over time to be typical performance at specified ages. For example, children who score "average" in reading readiness demonstrate behaviors typical for their age or grade level. "Below average" or "developmentally delayed" refers to performance typical of children in a younger age group than those being assessed.

It is possible to anchor standards in both criterion- and norm-referenced information for the same assessment. You start with a criterion-referenced scale, a scale describing performance relative to a clearly defined set of behaviors, then gather or otherwise obtain data about how a national, state, or local sample of students performed on the same measure. You can then say "Maria wrote a well-organized essay, receiving a '4' in organization; her performance was described as better than 75 percent of the students in the state." Or, on a more informal level, in your classroom, you can always describe an individual student's performance level in comparison to the rest of the class's performance: "Maria's score put her among the best in the class."

Some scales may look like absolute or criterion-referenced scales but might actually incorporate both norm- and criterion-referenced information. An age- or grade-related scale defines student performance in terms of benchmarks or expectations for a particular grade level. Benchmarks for 5th grade mathematics problem solving will differ from those for the 7th grade. What constitutes excellence in essay organization at the 8th grade will not do so at the 11th. Despite their "criterion-referenced" appearance, scales tied to an age or grade level curriculum have an underlying norm-referenced interpretation. The dimensions themselves were derived from what students were able to do at particular grades, not from absolute standards of performance across ages and grades. For practical purposes, these grade level scales are considered criterion referenced because their primary use is to decide what students can do vis-a-vis particular content and skills rather than to compare them to each other.

How can you get the best of both worlds? By determining appropriate standards according to your assessment purposes. For classroom or schoolwide assessment use, you'll probably lean toward criterion-referenced or absolute standards. For selection decisions in which there are more candidates than available space, you will probably use absolute standards for inclusion in the candidate pool, but normative standards for the final selection. For example, if you are selecting horn players for the after-school honors band, you will choose only the top 2 percent of the candidates.

We have not discussed how standards are set. How do you know where to set the acceptable level of performance? How good is competent? What is the cut point between barely satisfactory and satisfactory? High-stakes assessments, such as graduation certification, use formal standard-setting procedures. These may include using a group of judges, provided with norm- and criterion-referenced information, to determine a passing score. In district or schoolwide assessment, passing scores or labels describing poor and excellent performance are determined by consensus of those using the assessment. In the classroom, teachers set standards based on their experiences, their knowledge of what students have done in the past, their familiarity with expectations in a discipline, the current performance of students, and the purpose of the assessment.

Considering Other Choices:
Holistic or Analytic Criteria*

Based on experience with direct writing assessment, we offer two more choices in specifying criteria: holistic and analytic. Holistic criteria require raters to assign a single score based on the overall quality or to one aspect of the student's response. An analytic scale requires that raters give separate ratings to different aspects of the work. Criteria incorporating several outcomes are analytic.

---

*You may be familiar with the term "Primary Trait Scoring." When Primary Trait criteria focus on only one trait, they are holistic; when expanded to two or more traits, they become analytic.

Which Is Better?

By this time you know that we're going to say "it depends on the purpose of the assessment." The pattern of results from an analytic scale provides useful feedback about the strengths and weaknesses of the individual student and the classroom instructional program. Unfortunately, because student performance on different dimensions of an analytic scale may be related in complex ways, the results may not be as clearly diagnostic as desired. Despite the fact that one of the qualities of a good analytic scale, from an efficiency and measurement perspective, is that each dimension be distinct, the subscale scores are often highly interrelated and not well differentiated. CRESST research on analytic scoring scales found high correlations among scores for overall essay and paragraph organization, and between organization, support, and a general competence score. Under such circumstances, the diagnostic value of subscale performance is greatly diminished.

Holistic scoring is usually simpler and faster than analytic; an important concern when teacher time is involved. Unless assessment's purpose is not to provide data to guide program improvement, a quick overview of achievement may be particularly suitable for program evaluation, for flagging students who need more help, and for assigning final evaluations.

Concurrent use of analytic and holistic strategies can optimize both diagnostic value and efficiency. One approach emerging from minimum competency testing is to score all essays holistically then rate analytically those essays that were scored below minimum competency. Another strategy, used in the Maine statewide assessment, is to score essays holistically, but to note analytic dimensions that are particularly strong or weak in an individual's work as a kind of generic "comment" on the performance.

Opinions differ considerably regarding the value of these different approaches, and research is ongoing. The important point is not so much the correct labeling of scales, but that a variety of approaches exist and can prove useful.

What About Portfolio Assessment?

Portfolio assessment is often the first strategy that comes to mind when people think of alternative assessments. In some respects, portfolio assessment is a misnomer for "assessment of a body of work." In other instances, the portfolio assessment is really the assessment system.

Portfolios are collections of student work that are reviewed against criteria in order to judge an individual student or a program. The portfolio or collection of work does not constitute the assessment; it is simply a receptacle for work (essays, videotapes, art, journal entries, and so on) that may or may not be evaluated. The "assessment" in portfolio exists only when (1) an assessment purpose is defined; (2) criteria or methods for determining what is put into the portfolio, by whom, and when, are explicated; and (3) criteria for assessing either the collection or individual pieces of work are identified. Deciding what should be included is really a task description, not a scoring guideline problem. What goes in, who chooses, when samples are taken—these are dimensions of the assessment task that define the setting and kinds of work that will be considered. (See Chapter 7 for more discussion of portfolio assessment.)

There are two issues related to selecting the dimensions of scoring criteria for portfolio assessment: (1) What are the criteria for selecting the samples that go into the portfolio, and (2) What are the criteria for judging the quality of the samples? Prior to considering criteria for judging portfolios, you will need to determine whether the portfolio should be rated as a whole or as individual samples. Second, you need to decide which dimensions reflect the intent or purpose of your assessment. When looking at a body of work, many issues arise, for example:

- Will progress or improvement be assessed?
- How or will progress be evaluated?
- How will different tasks, videos, art work, essays, journal entries, and the like be compared or weighted in the assessment?
- What is the role of student reflection in the assessment? Parental input?

Once these issues are settled, defining the dimensions of portfolio scoring criteria is the same as defining multidimensional criteria. Perhaps the best known example of portfolio assessment criteria is provided by the Vermont Mathematics portfolio, which is summarized in Figure 5.10. A body of mathematics work is evaluated on two major dimensions, problem-solving and communication skill. Within each dimension, several subdimensions further define each of the larger skills. Ratings are given for the subskills under the two dimensions, problem solving and communication. You can see how this example of portfolio assessment criteria resembles the multidimensional examples in Figures 5.1 and 5.7.

Figure 5.10
Mathematics Rating Form

Student:: _____
ID Number: _____
School: _____
Grade: _____ Date: _____
Rater: _____

	A1 Understanding of Task	A2 How—Quality of Approaches/Procedures	A3 Why—Decisions Along the Way
	SOURCES OF EVIDENCE • Explanation of task • Reasonableness of approach • Correctness of response leading to inference of understanding	SOURCES OF EVIDENCE • Demonstrations • Descriptions (oral or written) • Drafts, scratch work, etc.	SOURCES OF EVIDENCE • Changes in approach • Explanations (oral or written) • Validation of final solution • Demonstration
ENTRY 1 Title: _____ P I A O Puzzle Investigation Application Other			
ENTRY 2 Title: _____ P I A O Puzzle Investigation Application Other			
ENTRY 3 Title: _____ P I A O Puzzle Investigation Application Other			
ENTRY 4 Title: _____ P I A O Puzzle Investigation Application Other			
ENTRY 5 Title: _____ P I A O Puzzle Investigation Application Other			
ENTRY 6 Title: _____ P I A O Puzzle Investigation Application Other			
ENTRY 7 Title: _____ P I A O Puzzle Investigation Application Other			
OVERALL RATINGS ↑			

UNDERSTANDING OF TASK
FINAL RATING
1 Totally misunderstood
2 Partially understood
3 Understood
4 Generalized, applied, extended

HOW—QUALITY OF APPROACHES/ PROCEDURES
FINAL RATING
1 Inappropriate or unworkable approach/ procedure
2 Appropriate approach/procedure some of the time
3 Workable approach/procedure
4 Efficient or sophisticated approach/procedure

WHY—DECISIONS ALONG THE WAY
FINAL RATING
1 No evidence of reasoned decision-making
2 Reasoned decision-making possible
3 Reasoned decisions/adjustments inferred with certainty
4 Reasoned decisions/adjustments shown/ explicated

Comments:

Figure 5.10 (continued)

A4 What—Outcomes of Activities	B1 Language of Mathematics	B2 Mathematical Representations	B3 Clarity of Presentation	CONTENT TALLIES
SOURCES OF EVIDENCE • Solutions • Extensions—observatons connections, applications syntheses, generalizations, abstractions	SOURCES OF EVIDENCE • Terminology • Notation/symbols	SOURCES OF EVIDENCE • Graphs, tables, charts • Models • Diagrams • Manipulatives	SOURCES OF EVIDENCE • Audio/video tapes (or transcripts) • Written work • Teacher interviews/observations • Journal entries • Student comments on cover sheet • Student self-assessment	Number Sense—Whole No./Fractions (4) Number Relationships/No. Theory (3) Operations/Place Value (4) Operations (8) Estimation (4/8) Patterns/Relationships (4) Patterns/Functions (8) Algebra (8) Geometry/Spatial Sense (4/8) Measurement (4/8) Statistics/Probability (4/8)

TASK CHARACTERISTICS

EMPOWERMENT COMMENTS

Motivation	Flexibility
Risk Taking	Reflecting
Confidence	Perseverance
Curiosity/Interest	Value Math

WHAT—OUTCOMES OF ACTIVITIES FINAL RATING	LANGUAGE OF MATHEMATICS FINAL RATING	MATHEMATICAL REPRESENTATIONS FINAL RATING	CLARITY OF PRESENTATION FINAL RATING
1 Solution without extensions 2 Solution with observations 3 Solution with connections or applications 4 Solution with synthesis generalization or abstraction	1 No or inappropriate use of mathematical language 2 Appropriate use of mathematical language some of the time 3 Appropriate use of mathematical language most of the time 4 Use of precise, elegant, appropriate mathematical language	1 No use of mathematical representation(s) 2 Use of mathematical representation(s) 3 Accurate and appropriate use of mathematical representation(s) 4 Perceptive use of mathematical representation(s)	1 Unclear (e.g., disorganized, incomplete, lacking detail) 2 Some clear parts 3 Mostly clear 4 Clear (e.g., well organized, complete, detailed)

Developing and Evaluating Scoring Criteria

Beginning the Development Process

The process for developing your own criteria is straightforward:

- Investigate how the assessed discipline defines quality performance.
- Gather sample rubrics for assessing writing, speech, the arts, and so on as models to adapt for your purposes.
- Gather samples of students' and experts' work that demonstrate the range of performance from ineffective to very effective.
- Discuss with others the characteristics of these models that distinguish the effective ones from the ineffective ones.
- Write descriptors for the important characteristics.
- Gather another sample of students' work.
- Try out criteria to see if they help you make accurate judgments about students.
- Revise your criteria.
- Try it again until the rubric score captures the "quality" of the work.

You probably noticed how recurrent this development process is. Initial ideas about important and scorable aspects of student performance become refined through use. Your criteria may focus on process—how a student approaches and solves a problem—as well as on the product or outcomes.

For example, we can refer to the development process for the criteria in Figure 5.5 (Baker, Aschbacher, Niemi, and Sato 1992). CRESST developed its rubric for rating depth of content understanding in history by collecting and examining the differences in essays written by history experts (university professors and graduate students in history) versus those written by novices (high school students). CRESST researchers looked for dimensions that seemed to differentiate the performance of these two groups. In a number of subject areas, the researchers observed differences between the students and the experts in the application of prior knowledge, the use of organizing concepts and principles, and misconceptions. These traits defined the first draft of scoring criteria. The criteria were then tried out on samples of student work and further clarified and refined to ensure that the scales were clearly defined, were appropriate for the range of student responses likely to be encountered, and enabled teachers or other raters to distinguish between essays that deserved adjacent points on a scale.

While undertaking the task of developing criteria, don't forget to take advantage of others' work. Quite often you can import or modify criteria from state and local assessment programs, curriculum experts, or colleagues who have grappled with similar assessment problems. Research literature on alternative assessment also provides examples of pilot alternative assessments similar to the one appearing in Figure 5.4, which can be adapted for classroom use. There is also a small but growing literature on the nature of expertise in various disciplines, such as how an historian reads and uses primary source documents.

Evaluating Criteria

Your criteria for judging students' work shape the decisions you eventually make about programs and students. Regardless of whether you are developing your own criteria or using those provided by others, it is important to review the quality of the scoring guidelines. We conclude this chapter with a proposed set of "criteria for criteria"— a checklist you can use to rate the quality of scoring criteria you borrow or develop. Our proposed criteria appear in Figure 5.11.

Now let's look at a set of dimensions for assessing the worth of your own criteria.

Keyed to Important Outcomes

At a minimum, criteria for judging student performance need to address all the student outcomes you are trying to measure. For example, your criteria for judging student drama productions should encompass all the important drama and art that you want to be able to assess, and no others. If originality and logical presentation are part of the desired outcomes, you will want to include scales for judging these aspects of student work. If they are not an important outcome, omit them.

Sensitive to Purpose

What educational decisions will you make on the basis of your assessment? The answer to this question should guide your decisions about whether to use a checklist or rating scales, how many scales, which traits, what types of scale, and so forth. Do you need a global, holistic view of student achievement or an analytical one that gives you information about several specific aspects of students achievement? Do you need the information in the form of a number for ease of reporting and aggregation at the expense of detail, or do you need the richness of qualitative description, or perhaps both?

Figure 5.11
How Do You Evaluate Scoring Criteria?

❐   All important outcomes are addressed by criteria.

❐   Rating strategy matches decision purpose: holistic for global, evaluative view; analytic for diagnostic view.

❐   Rating scale provides usable, easily interpreted score.

❐   Criteria employ concrete references, clear language understandable to students, parents, other teachers.

❐   Criteria reflect current conceptions of "excellence" accepted in the field.

❐   Criteria have been reviewed for developmental, ethnic, gender bias.

❐   Criteria reflect teachable outcomes.

❐   Criteria are limited to feasible number of dimensions.

❐   Criteria are generalizable to other similar tasks or larger performance domain.

Meaningful, Clear, and Credible

The criteria by which you judge a performance need to be meaningful to students, parents, raters, teachers, administrators, policymakers, and the public. If the criteria are not credible, the results will probably be ignored or may be misused. Examples of student work that illustrate criterion traits can help make the criteria concrete for others. Involving others in the development of criteria increases their credibility.

Because one of the tenets of performance assessment is public and discussed criteria, your criteria need to make sense to students so that they will be able to apply them easily to their own work and become self-regulated learners. Although judgments of student performance tend to be subjective by their nature, they are more reliable and credible when they rely less on high inference and more on observable, concrete characteristics.

Fair and Unbiased

Not only do assessment tasks need to be fair, but so do the criteria by which you define excellence. Unrecognized biases can seep into your definitions of traits, your specifications for what kind of performance earns which scale point, and your application of those criteria to individual pieces of student work. When you want your criteria to have diagnostic value, they must be sensitive to instruction and students' opportunities to learn the skills that are assessed. In contrast, you do not want them to reflect variables over which educators have no control, such as a child's culture, sex, or socioeconomic background.

Feasible

Several reasons exist to limit the number and complexity of the performance dimensions to be judged. First, the time, effort, and money available for judging performance are always limited, sometimes severely so. Second, raters find it difficult to address too many different aspects of a work at once. In our experience at CRESST, raters were frustrated when asked to use more than six or seven scales for rating student essays. It became an onerous task and a less reliable process. Third, students will probably find it difficult to deal with too many aspects of their work at once. And finally, administrators and policymakers usually need information in as brief a form as possible. Separate scores for a large number of traits or for complex characteristics may make it more difficult to use the results effectively.

Generalizable

Although we recognize that criteria for performance are strongly linked to discipline-based notions of excellence, rating can be more efficient when a single set of "generic" criteria can serve multiple topics, tasks, or disciplines. For example, we could develop a common set of criteria for assessing student understanding of science concepts through journals, hands-on experimentation, computer simulation, and oral presentation. We could also use a common set of criteria for judging student essays in social studies, science, and math? As disparate as these situations may seem, it is possible to envelop generic criteria for some purposes. If we could conceptualize excellence in consistent ways across assessment methods and disciplines, our criteria could have a more powerful impact on learning and instruction. Our example of the CRESST history-social studies rubric (Figure 5.5), which has also been applied to science and economics, shows one strategy for developing cross-discipline criteria. Like all good criteria, these proposed dimension are subject to revision and refinement.

References

Baker, E.L., P.R. Aschbacher, D. Niemi, and E. Sato. (1992). *CRESST Performance Assessment Models: Assessing Content Area Explanations.* Los Angeles: University of California, Center for Research on Evaluation, Standards, and Student Testing.

Baxter, G., R.J. Shavelson, S. Goldman, and J. Pine. (Spring 1992). *Journal of Educational Measurement* 29, 1: 1-17.

Jones, E., and J.M. Roberts. (1990). *Profile of Developmental Outcomes for Kindergarten Literacy and Numeracy Skills.* Soledad, Calif.: San Vincente School District.

Vermont Department of Education. (1992). *Looking Beyond "the Answer": The Report of Vermont's Mathematics Portfolio Assessment Program, Pilot Year 1990-91.* Montpellier: Vermont Department of Education.

6

Ensuring Reliable Scoring

A fundamental feature of performance-based assessment is its reliance on human judgment. As any trial lawyer will attest, two people viewing the same occurrence or reading the same document often come up with conflicting perceptions or interpretations. Likewise, persons viewing the same behavior on different occasions may arrive at different judgments about that behavior. The user or developer of alternative assessments must seek to minimize such differences; otherwise the measures cannot be fair, consistent, or valid. Sound scoring procedures help the process.

Understanding the Importance of Reliability and Consistency

The most obvious reason for consistent scoring is equity. To be meaningful, judgments of student performance cannot be capricious. You need to have confidence that the grade or judgment was a result of the actual performance, not some superficial aspect of the product or scoring situation. Was Yuki's grade unduly influenced by her spelling? Did Mark get a better (or worse) grade because his project was graded near the end when you were tired? How was Jamal's grade affected by the fact that another teacher did part of the scoring? What about Corinne? Did she fail the competency writing test this year because the raters were more stringent than last year?

Inconsistency is especially troublesome when the results influence important decisions about students or programs. What grade does Denisha deserve? Should Marta be allowed to take the Advanced Placement English class despite low standardized test scores? Should the school's new math program continue? Even when the results of a single assessment do not carry high stakes, inconsistency means inaccurate scoring. More to the point: inconsistent scoring means the scores have little meaning. If an "A" doesn't consistently represent excellent performance, then what does it mean? The best in the class? The best of a poor lot? Improved effort? If a performance or project receives different scores from different judges, what does each really mean? Which one is accurate? If you apply criteria differently depending on how long you've been scoring, what does the final set of scores mean? What does an individual's score mean?

Achieving Consistency

Equitable and meaningful scoring requires informed and consistent judgment. How do you avoid capricious subjectivity? As we discussed in Chapter 5, having well-defined and defensible criteria for judging student performance goes a long way toward achieving consistent scoring, but there are other conditions that must be met to ensure consistent scoring. First, those making judgments—you, teacher colleagues, the state department of education—must thoroughly understand the criteria in a similar fashion. A consensus among raters about the meaning of the criteria and how they are to be applied builds the foundation for scoring consistency. Second, you need a system for monitoring the consistency of ratings over the period in which performance is being judged. This consistency has several facets. Two or more judges rating the same performance should have general agreement. One judge should rate a particular performance in much the same way regardless of when it is observed—whether during the beginning of the day, somewhere in the middle, or near the end. Judges should rate the same performances similarly on separate occasions. And, the same performances rated on two separate occasions by two different group of judges should be rated similarly. If your scores are used to make high-stakes decisions such as promotion, graduation, or special class placement, you should formally document evidence of scoring consistency.

Professional Development Benefits

The process by which judges learn to apply scoring criteria in a consistent manner can provide a valuable opportunity for professional development. Rater training helps teachers come to a consensual definition of key aspects of student performance. This can lead to a reprioritization of classroom goals as well as insight about the strengths and weaknesses of their students' performances. The scoring process can provide a model for classroom assessment and encourage more collaboration among teachers in the appraisal of student outcomes.

To reap the benefits of consistency and professional growth, you will need good training procedures and a carefully structured rating process. This chapter outlines major considerations in devising and implementing a valid scoring procedure. Although the process we describe has its origin in formal, high-stakes assessments at the district and state level, keep in mind that consistent scoring applies to all forms of assessment, be they classroom grades or college admissions. Decisions about a student can't be valid unless based on reliable information.

Rater Training:
A Prerequisite for Consistent Scoring

There are a number of ways to achieve consistency. Our approach emphasizes training raters to a common standard because this approach is efficient and provides teachers with instructionally useful information. Other approaches devote less attention to rater training and consensus-building and rely on multiple judgments of student work to achieve a similar result. As you might expect, the approach you choose depends on your assessment purpose and available resources.

During rater training, judges learn what the scoring criteria mean, what aspects of performance each is intended to capture, and what each of the scale points represents. It is during the training session that you make sure raters apply the criteria consistently to a range of student work samples. This is also the time when raters learn how to record their scores.

Training Manuals

Formal scoring manuals can be very helpful both during and after training. For large-scale assessments, such as yearly district or state testing programs, a scoring manual provides an "institutional memory" of assessment procedures and serves as a useful reference for interpreting scores. For high-stakes classroom assessments, such as Advanced Placement "screening" examinations, or an algebra readiness test, scoring manuals can be useful in discussions with parents or students who want to know how scores are achieved or improved. Typical scoring guides include:

- Fully explicated scoring criteria;

- Examples or models illustrating each score point;

- An abbreviated, one-page, version of the criteria or reference during actual rating; and

- A sample form for recording scores.

You might want to review training manuals from several sources before designing your own rater training. If you are interested in a detailed description of the rater training process, a complete scoring manual developed by the Riverside Publishing Company appears in *Educational Performance Assessment*, edited by Fred Finch (1991). State departments of education are also sources of published scoring manuals.

Training Procedures

Actual rater training is designed to create a consensual understanding of the scoring criteria, provide extensive practice in actual scoring, and, in the case of high-takes assessment, document acceptable levels of scoring consistency (reliability). During rater training, practice scoring sessions provide raters immediate, substantive feedback about their judgments and ample opportunities to ask questions. Raters also come to understand that their job is to make a judgment based on the scoring rubric, not to revise or criticize the rubric and then follow their own inclinations. Without such an understanding, an entire assessment enterprise can be sabotaged.

A typical training session includes:

- **Orientation to the assessment task.** Raters receive an overview of the assessment context, what the results will be used for, who will use them, what directions and prompts the students received, and how the scoring guide operationalizes desired outcomes or processes. It is common to ask raters to actually take the test as a means of orienting them to the scoring task.

- **Clarification of the scoring criteria.** In this phase of training, raters engage in extensive discussion. Both the criteria dimensions and scale values are defined and a range of models provided to exemplify each. Discussion often moves from simpler judgments, such as which samples illustrate high, medium, or low performances, to more difficult distinctions required for assigning numerical scores.

- **Practice scoring.** This is the heart of the rater training process. At first, sample assessments are scored one at a time with discussion following each paper. As raters become more fluent with the scoring guide, they get opportunities to exercise more difficult judgments with problematic (atypical) or borderline assessments.

- **Protocol revision.** During the discussion and practice scoring, raters naturally devise certain rules for dealing with the unanticipated aspects of judgment posed by a particular set of papers and not covered by the scoring guide. For example, when almost every student has misinterpreted the test prompt in the same fashion, rather than to score all answers as "off topic" or "unacceptable," raters may decide to assign scores based on the student-defined task. Or, if many traits are to be scored, raters may decide that different raters should specialize in scoring a few of the traits rather than having all raters score every sample on every dimension.

- **Score recording.** For all assessments, student scores must be recorded in some fashion, on the roll sheet or on summary sheets for a classroom, grade level, or school. Rater training covers the format for recording scores and any special procedures for calculating student scores such as averaging and totalling across dimensions.

- **Documenting rater reliability.** Rater training ends when there is agreement that scorers have reached an acceptable level of consistency, usually rating sample pieces within one point of each other. In order to determine when raters are ready for the real thing, reliability checks are conducted during training. Figure 6.1 provides an example of how to check rater consistency using the percent agreement method.

- **Scheduling Considerations.** How much time will it take to train raters to an acceptable level of agreement before letting them judge student work? It depends on:

    — How experienced your raters are.
    — Whether they are familiar with your scoring criteria.

— How quickly raters come to consensus about the meaning of the criteria.

— The complexity of the scoring criteria, and the quality of the work to be judged—with borderline work being the most difficult to assess quickly.

We have found that it takes about three to four hours to train raters to use a holistic or simple (two- to four-trait) analytic scale. More complex scales can require up to a full day of training.

Rater fatigue is an important factor in scoring; we consider a six-hour session a full day's work. You should also schedule time for retraining or refreshing raters at the beginning of each new scoring day, and certainly for any changes in topics or tasks that use the same scoring

Figure 6.1
Calculating Rater Agreement
(Three raters for two papers)

Rater	Is Rater in Perfect Agreement with the Criterion Score?			Is Rater in Agreement with the Criterion Score, Plus or Minus 1 Point?		
	Paper #1	Paper #2	Rater's Average Agreement	Paper #1	Paper #2	Rater's Average Agreement
Linda	yes	no	50%	yes	no	50%
Robert	no	no	0%	yes	yes	100%
Ella	yes	yes	100%	yes	yes	100%
Total	67% = yes	33% = yes	50%	100% = yes	67% = yes	83%

Figure 6.1 illustrates the case in which three raters are asked to rate two criterion papers after some training. According to the results in the figure, Linda agrees with the criterion score for paper 1 but not for paper 2; in fact, for paper 2 she is not even within one point of the criterion score. Robert is not in perfect agreement with the criterion scores on either paper 1 or paper 2 but is in agreement plus-or-minus one score point on both papers. Ella is in agreement all the time and is ready to rate student work. Robert and Linda probably need a little more training. Paper 2 causes more problems for raters than paper 1, so further training should focus on distinguishing the criterion score from neighboring scale points. In reporting these results you could say, "On average, raters obtained perfect agreement with criterion scores 50 percent of the time, and reached ±1 agreement 83 percent of the time.

criteria. In high-stakes assessment, retraining often takes place after any lengthy breaks such as lunch.

Training Paper Issues

Because rater training provides a dry run for actual scoring, it behooves you to anticipate as many possible sources of rater disagreement as possible before rater training and to build opportunities into the training papers for eliciting disagreement and discussing it. For example, the syntactical constructions used by non-native English speakers raise issues related to balancing content with communication concerns. You should also deal with handwriting and legibility issues or aesthetic quality concerns in visual and performing arts. Finally, you want to be sure that the sample papers you select for training represent not only each point on the score distribution but also the entire range of student performance likely to be encountered in scoring. The natural human tendency is to grade normatively. The better work samples from a set of relatively poor papers may receive higher scores than they would were they part of a stack of relatively good papers. The reverse can also be the case. This tendency should be discussed during rater training with examples provided so that the scoring criteria maintain the same meaning across different sets of papers and different scoring occasions.

Obtaining Sample and Check Papers

Because a wide array of sample work is needed to guide raters, you should collect samples from a diverse group of students. Pick work from a field-test, a previous assessment, or from the actual assessment. To identify appropriate training and check papers, a group of "experts"— teachers from the grades and subjects involved who are familiar with your scoring criteria—can be quite helpful. They can select examples that illustrate the range of responses, from clear to borderline, for each score point so that raters will be trained to handle all situations. If several prompts or tasks are used in the assessment, examples need to be drawn for each. If you are using age-related scales across grade levels, you need examples to illustrate each age level. It is also useful to prepare comment sheets explaining how the specific aspects of each piece of work represent criteria for a particular score. The expert group can then identify samples that will be used for (1) training discussions, (2) practice, and (3) checking consistency.

Score Recording Concerns

You need to provide raters a method for recording student scores. In your own classroom, you might simply record scores at the top of the student's paper and then in your roll book. Some teachers use the scoring criteria as a feedback sheet for students. They circle deficient areas or note strengths using the descriptors on the guide. The same process can be used to create a classroom profile on one master scoring guide.

In more formal assessment settings, score sheets become a matter of public record and are used to provide feedback to teachers and others. Data analysts also use them to calculate test statistics. In these instances, raters are often given machine readable documents for "bubbling" in student scores as well as other important information such as the school, district, student, and rater identification numbers and the code numbers for topic or task and date. Whenever you have two or more raters scoring student work, you'll need to remind them not to indicate scores, comments, or corrections on the sample itself. You don't want a subsequent rating influenced by their comments.

Reliability Issues

The purpose of rater training is to create consistent, reliable scoring procedures. Thus, a method of determining if raters are consistent should be built into the training period. Many strategies for checking rater reliability exist. One commonly employed approach is to prepare in advance and score a set of ten or so "reliability check" papers representing the range of student performance. Ask the raters to score this same set and compare their judgments with you or others who are trusted assessors. Reasonable agreement with both the expert judgments and with each other suggests that raters are ready to score actual student work.

What constitutes reasonable agreement? You can ask that all raters be in exact agreement before you consider them reliable, or you can use the less stringent "plus or minus one" rule, which is fairly common and says that raters are "in agreement" if they agree within one scale point, "plus or minus." For example, if the score on a particular reliability-check sample is a "3," anyone who gave it a rating of "2", "3," or "4" is considered to be on target.

Regardless of the target level of agreement you choose, when you train raters, the goal is to have them apply the scoring criteria exactly as intended, not to within one scale point of the target score. When a rater has difficulty applying the criteria exactly as intended, you should spend time during training discussing the practice papers, criteria, and decision rules for applying the criteria in order to bring the rater up to an acceptable level of consistency. However, some raters may not be able to adjust their internal criteria to match the scoring guides. These aberrant scorers should be dismissed or assigned to other tasks during actual scoring.

In addition to deciding how close ratings should be to establish consistency, you need to think about how often they need to be in such agreement. If you are asking for exact agreement, which can be difficult to obtain, your criterion for reliability may be less stringent than if you are using the "plus or minus one" rule. At CRESST, we often ask that raters agree with the experts at least 90 percent of the time on each scoring dimension when using the "one point off" guideline. The guideline for exact agreement could drop to 75 to 80 percent under the more stringent condition. The actual percentage of agreement varies depending on the assessment purpose and stakes involved.

Regardless of how you define "rater agreement," the purpose of reliability checks is to ensure that student scores aren't the result of capricious judgment, one of the most commonly cited arguments against performance assessment. Consider the classic study conducted by Paul Deidrich (1963) at the Educational Testing Service in which the same essay was assigned an entire range of scores by a group of raters. What most don't remember about this study is that acceptable levels of rater agreement were obtained when the judges (1) were drawn from the same discipline, (2) used explicit scoring criteria, and (3) participated in a training session.

Ensuring Equitable Judgments During an Actual Scoring Session

Maintaining Consistency

Documenting rater consistency during training is simply the first step toward creating a fair, equitable scoring process. Because the purpose of rater training is to develop rater consistency, you need to monitor rater scoring patterns during the actual scoring process as well. Research shows that raters have a tendency to drift away from formal criteria to their own, more idiosyncratic views (Quellmalz and Burry 1983). Human judgments and expectations are shaped not only by formal standards, such as scoring criteria, but also by their prior experience and the actual range of performance currently being assessed. If the entire set of performances appear to be relatively "poor" according to the objective criteria, raters develop a tendency to shift the criteria downward so they can award higher scores to the "best of the worst" papers. As a teacher, you too have perhaps been aware that your standards and expectations for students change during the grading process. You modify your ideas somewhat after looking at several pieces of student work. For this reason, training sessions need to include a large sample of papers and the entire range that might be encountered during actual scoring.

For classroom assessment purposes, you can check your consistency by stopping midway and rescoring some of the first student work you scored. When you are scoring several different dimensions or topics, you can score all work on one dimension or related to one topic at the same time, then go back and score for other factors. Scoring all papers several times, once for each different dimension or topic, is often quicker than going through individual papers for everything at once and applying multiple criteria or reading different kinds of responses. Your scoring pace also increases as you become familiar with the criteria.

For school-level, larger-scale, or high-stakes assessment, you'll want to build in more formal rater consistency checks. For essay scoring this is sometimes done by burying pre-scored common check papers at designated intervals in each rater's stack of papers. The scoring director then checks raters on the common paper and works with those who have drifted away from a consistent application of the scoring guide. Another method is to conduct mini-training sessions first thing in the morning or right after lunch. Raters score a common set of check papers, much as they did in training. Those who have drifted from the preset standard (exact agreement; plus or minus one point) participate in a review session and are rechecked before being allowed to continue scoring.

An additional consistency consideration in large-scale assessment relates to lack of bias in rater judgments. You need to be sure that raters working together don't form subgroups who agree with each other but not all the other participating raters. To avoid this, break up rater groups at periodic intervals and have second ratings of papers/work done by raters assigned to other tables or physical locations.

Managing Logistics

Although achieving consistent judgment is the overriding concern of scoring, conducting a scoring session involves a number of logistical and technical issues. Scheduling is one of the most fundamental concerns in planning a scoring session. As people tend to tire in the afternoon and rate more slowly, you might consider scheduling your rating sessions early and avoiding the late afternoon. Access to a copy machine enables you to address any unanticipated shortages of rating materials or to reproduce papers that require discussion during the rating session. Further, rating is an intense activity; provide frequent breaks and snacks (lots of fruit and carbohydrates, little sugar). The scoring area itself should be quiet and comfortable with ample room for raters to accommodate the work to be reviewed. A rater's nightmare is to work in the gym on folding chairs and tables at 3:30 on a hot May afternoon during band practice.

Another concern is managing the flow of papers or other student products. In large-scale assessments, each table of scorers should have their own leader whose sole duty is to manage the paper flow and monitor rater consistency. Our experience suggests that bundles of student work that take about one hour to rate are easier for raters to handle than individual pieces. The number of pieces in each bundle will vary with the nature of the task and the complexity of the scoring scheme. In writing assessments, for example, sets often consist of fifteen to twenty-five papers, whereas a bundle of portfolios might include only four to six. Regardless of how work is bundled, individual pieces must be randomly assigned to bundles and bundles randomly assigned to raters so that no systematic scoring effects occur. For formal assessments, both raters and students should be assigned identification numbers to guard against bias and protect privacy.

You'll need to decide whether to mix different grade levels or different topics together in the same scoring session. Generally, this is not done unless the purpose of an assessment is to compare students at different grade levels on the same scoring scale. In large-scale assessments, different topics are either assigned to different rater groups or scored separately from each other with a session of refresher training preceding the topic change.

Another concern that can cause problems later if not monitored carefully is ensuring that scorers are recording required information properly. Were all identification numbers bubbled in along with the scores? Were scores recorded for all papers rated? Do all students have scores? The list is extensive. Try to anticipate what can go wrong and devise strategies for either preventing it from happening or for fixing it.

Ensuring Technical Quality

Advice on all the technical decisions you have make to ensure scoring accuracy and equity is beyond the scope of this book and in fact constitutes a psychometrician's career. If you are assessing for a high-stakes decision, especially if that decision can get you sued, disparaged on page one of your local newspaper, or called before the board of education, you may want to bring in a technical consultant to structure your scoring process and help you document the reliability of student scores. Following are some of the questions you need to address:

How many raters are needed? This, of course, depends on how much work is rated, how many ratings each piece will receive, how long it takes to rate each piece, and how many days are available for scoring. Holistic scoring of one-to-two page essays generally goes quickly, sometimes as quickly as a minute a paper. A complex analytic rating on longer pieces can take four to five minutes per paper. Portfolios can take longer still. As for the number of days, our experience suggests raters can get quite burned out after four or five days.

How many scores per paper? Effective training and vigilant monitoring of the scoring process can eliminate much of the need to do multiple scoring of the same dimension of student work. Multiple raters are needed for each paper when raters are inexperienced or there is little evidence that raters are using the same criteria and standards in making their judgments. The need for multiple scores depends on your assessment purpose. The more serious the consequences, the more important it is that you document consistency. Our experience suggests that no more than two raters are needed for any piece; the ratings can be summed or averaged to provide a final score. A third opinion can be called in for difficult cases, such as the occasional nightmare paper that draws both the lowest and highest score.

In some situations, one score is sufficient for a majority of the pieces. Consider a situation in which selection, placement, or other critical decisions about individual students will be made based on some prespecified standard or cut score. If your training and scoring check papers show that raters are consistent, the only papers requiring two or more ratings will be those borderline papers falling around the passing score. Because rating is an expensive process, you will need to balance reliability concerns against those for cost and efficiency.

How are papers scored for evaluation purposes? If student scores will be used for program evaluation rather than individual assessment, a reliable estimate of an individual student score is less critical than the average score for the task. Most pieces of work can be read only once, and your reliability evidence can be obtained on a sample of work (perhaps 20 percent), which is rated by two or more raters. If you are using student samples to evaluate a program and don't have to provide individual scores to teachers, it is more efficient to score a randomly selected sample of student work. Your technical consultant can advise you about sample size and the appropriate manner of selection.

Providing Evidence of Reliability

For high-stakes assessments, you need to formally document the consistency and reliability of your scoring process. Plan to invest in the services of a technical expert in advance of the scoring to ensure that you have an adequate scoring design, that you are collecting suitable evidence, and that your data are appropriately formatted to ease data analysis.

The following are some relevant sources of evidence:

- **Results of the qualifying check after training.** Plan to report on what agreement level was required. What proportion of your raters passed on the first try? What was the average level of agreement among those passing?

- **Results of the consistency check during scoring.** Plan to report on what agreement level was required. How many and when were the checks made? What proportion of your raters passed without remediation? What was the average level of agreement on the checks?

- **Inter-rater reliability results for student work scored by more than one rater.** Percentage agreement among raters and generalizability coefficients are two frequently used techniques. Each of these is calculated separately for each scale you use. As a guide, you need to double score at least 20 percent of your student samples to get sufficient evidence, and if more than two raters are involved, you need to consult a statistician for help with a balanced design specifying which raters are to score which pieces of student work.

What level of agreement or reliability is high enough? Of course the answer is: it depends on the decisions you are making. The more critical or restrictive the consequences are, the more reliable your scores need to be. In general, reliability coefficients of .70 and above are considered respectable. Coefficients of .90 and above are not uncommon with standardized multiple-choice tests, and large-scale direct writing assessments.

- **Rater consistency across years.** When you want to be sure that your rating scale is consistent from year to year—for example, when results are being used in state assessments to track trends over time—you need to include with this year's scoring a sufficient sample of student work from last year's scoring. Agreement in scores assigned can then be checked, and if necessary, statistical adjustments can be made for differences.

- **Rater consistency across different locations or different groups of raters.** Similar to checking consistency across years, if student work is to be scored at a number of different locations or by different groups of raters, you need to check on the consistency of these different groups. For example, a state might convene four regional workshops to score its hands-on science assessments, or a district assessment might require each school to score its own students' work. One way to check for consistency would be to seed the work scored by each group with a common set of work. At scoring site one, for instance, scorers would assess student work assigned specifically to site one plus the common set; site two scores would assess student work assigned specifically to site two plus the common set and so forth. Scores on the common set can then be checked for consistency.

- **Inter-rater consistency.** This is the degree to which one rater remains consistent over time. Check for this by having raters score the same piece more than once at different points in the scoring process.

Checking the Reliability of Your Rating Process

As a summary of many of the issues covered in this chapter, use the following checklist to see if your scoring procedures are sound and reliable. Do you have:

[ ] documented, field-tested scoring guide
[ ] clear, concrete criteria
[ ] annotated examples of all score points

[ ] ample practice and feedback for raters
[ ] multiple raters with demonstrated agreement prior to scoring
[ ] periodic reliability checks throughout
[ ] retraining when necessary
[ ] arrangements for collection of suitable reliability data

References

Baker, E.L., P.R. Aschbacher, D. Niemi, and E. Sato. (1992). *CRESST Performance Assessment Models: Assessing Content Area Explanations.* Los Angeles: University of California, Center for Research on Evaluation, Standards, and Student Testing.

Deidrich, P.B. (1963). "The Measurement of Skill in Writing." *School Review* 54: 584-592.

Finch, F. (1991). *Educational Performance Assessment.* Chicago: Riverside Publishing Company.

Quellmalz, E., and J. Burry. (1983). "Analytic Scales for Assessing Students' Expository and Narrative Writing Skills." (CSE Resource Paper No. 5). Los Angeles: University of California, Center for Research on Evaluation, Standards, and Students Testing.

7

Using Alternative Assessment for Decision Making

We have considered a number of important issues in the development of good alternative assessments: What is alternative assessment? How do we identify suitable assessment tasks? What should criteria include? What do sound scoring procedures look like? We now turn to the reason we've developed alternative assessments in the first place: to make appropriate decisions about students and programs.

This is a critically important point: assessment is not an end in itself. Rather, assessment provides information for decision making about what students have learned, what grades are deserved, whether students should pass on to the next grade, what groups they should be assigned to, what help they need, what areas of classroom instruction need revamping, where the school curriculum needs bolstering, and so forth. Good assessment enables us to accurately characterize students' functioning and performance and to make sound decisions that will improve education.

Does using the results of an assessment contribute to good decisions? This is the crux of how we judge the quality of an assessment. Policymakers and the public have placed considerable faith in standardized tests, in their quality, and their efficient ability to lead us to accurate conclusions about students and schools. Unfortunately, some believe that this faith in testing has been misplaced. As we have become more sophisticated consumers of assessment, we have raised more questions about what these tests actually tell us. Do Scholastic Aptitude Test scores really predict which students will be successful in college? If not, how much weight should they be given in college admission decisions? Do state assessments give schools the kind of information they need to improve their programs? Do they help policymakers and the public know whether students are learning what they need to know and be able to do? Do multiple-choice tests allow students to demonstrate their full understanding of a subject? If not, how much should we be relying on them when making decisions about students and programs?

Dissatisfaction with traditional tests has encouraged teachers and entire states to embrace alternative forms of assessment. But alternative formats alone cannot guarantee good assessment. We need to apply to alternative assessments the same scrutiny that allowed us to see the limitations, as well as the strengths, of more traditional tests. We need to be sure that the assessments we plan to use are helping and not hurting students, programs, and schools.

This chapter highlights issues that should be considered when using assessments, alternative or otherwise. We begin with an overview of two key concepts in assessing the quality of any assessment: validity and reliability. We then examine three major questions guiding appropriate use of assessment information:

1. How does your decision context and intended use influence your concerns for the quality of your assessment program?

2. How do you ensure that an assessment is giving you good information for decision making?

3. How can you use your assessment results to improve instruction?

Note that we address issues of assessment quality before we provide concrete examples of how to use assessment results. We do this to emphasize that *assessment quality is always an issue* and should be considered before actually using results. If an assessment does not provide good information for decision making, its use may constitute misuse.

Before venturing further, we remind you that for purposes of simplicity throughout this book we have examined issues from the perspective of a single assessment. No doubt you are well aware that no single assessment or test constitutes a sound assessment strategy. All assessments, even the very best, are imperfect and fallible. Alternative assessments, like all assessments, should be used in concert with other sources of information to constitute a systematic and balanced assessment program. As you read about factors influencing test use, keep in mind that the same concerns that apply to an individual assessment are applicable to a collection of assessments or an entire system of assessment.

Issues in Ensuring Quality—
Validity and Reliability

Does an assessment provide accurate information for decision making? Do its results permit accurate and fair conclusions about student performance? Does using the results contribute to sound decisions? These are the central issues in judging the quality of an assessment. If we wish to answer these questions in the affirmative, our assessments must be both reliable and valid—terms the measurement community uses to address these same concerns.

Reliability: Stability of Performance

Earlier, we introduced the concept of reliability as it relates to the consistency of human judgments. We have seen that there are several ways to ensure acceptable levels of rater agreement about student performance. However, reliability in the larger sense refers to whether test scores retain their meaning (remain consistent) despite superficial changes in the assessment situation—from one day to the next, regardless of the person judging the performance or the day or time at which assessments are scored. If Maria writes a critique of *Tristam Shandy* today, tomorrow, or next Tuesday, we expect her performance to be essentially the same on all three occasions. If her teacher reads her paper tonight, tomorrow, or next Tuesday, we expect the teacher to give her the same grade or to draw the same conclusions about how her skills have developed and about her strengths and weakness. If Byron is able to create two approaches for answering a mathematics problem today, we expect him to be able to come up with a similar analysis of a similar problem on Friday or next week. Without such consistency, we cannot say with any confidence that we know what a student can do. An unreliable test score is useless because it does not tell us anything meaningful or generalizable about student performance. For this reason, we must ensure that our results are reliable before we concern ourselves with validity, the issue closest to test use. In fact, most of us at one time learned the maxim, "to be valid, a test score must be reliable." When asked to recall this truism, many of us aren't sure whether reliability precedes validity or vice versa. Perhaps the easiest way to keep the relationship straight is to remember that for a score to be valuable (validity) for decision making, it must be repeatable (reliable).

Validity: Accuracy of Test-based Conclusions

Measurement specialists know that although reliability is necessary, it is not a sufficient condition for validity—in other words, whether a test score yields accurate conclusions about a student's performance and is subsequently a sound basis for decisions. A test result could be perfectly reliable but not very relevant to the decision for which it is intended. To take an extreme example, a test for typing or word processing may give you highly reliable (repeatable and consistent) information for judging a student's keyboarding skills and speed, but these results are useless for making decisions about the student's writing ability. Similarly, a multiplication test may give you highly consistent results about your students' computation skills, but be of limited use in determining whether they are successful problem solvers.

Determining the validity of an assessment depends on how you plan to use it. Throughout this book, we have used the word "validity" somewhat loosely, as though it were a quality or characteristic of a particular test. In fact, assessments themselves are neither valid nor invalid; their validity depends on the purposes for which they are used. We assess the validity of a test by determining whether or not a *conclusion* based on the test score is accurate for a particular use or purpose. For example, if we wish to use the results of a test to identify students who have mastered linear equations we ask, "Do the scores identify all the students who have mastered linear equations?" or "Do the students identified as those who need more help actually have such a need?" More precisely, when we speak of the validity of the test to identify masters of linear equations, we are really referring to the *evidence* we have that tells us our score-based conclusions are correct, that students who score at or above our passing score have actually mastered the content. We have little reason to use results and can have little confidence in doing so until we have corroborating evidence, such as student performance on subsequent assignments, performance on similar kinds of assessments, teacher observation, and other teacher judgments that support our score-based conclusions.

Because it is somewhat unwieldy to repeat this precise definition, we shall continue to use "validity" to stand for "evidence to support score-based inferences." As you are reading, keep in mind the more accurate definition.

Remember, too, that assessments can be valid for some purposes but inappropriate for others. For example, a survey test of basic skills provides useful comparisons with a national sample but may be relatively worthless for pinpointing mastery of local curricular objectives. The results of a final exam may be valid for determining whether a student should receive an "A" or a "B" in a class, yet it may not be valid for identifying the students who would benefit most from accelerated instruction or the select few who can participate in the new gifted program. The lesson here is that if a test claims to have multiple uses, it should be accompanied by evidence to support each separate use. What kind of evidence is that? The next section provides you with things to think about when determining what kinds of formal evidence you will want to consider when using assessments to make decisions about students, classrooms, or schools.

How Does Decision Context and Intended Use Affect Concerns for Quality?

Know Your Assessment Purpose

Assessments are created to provide information for making decisions about students, classrooms, schools, districts, states, and national education goals. What is the purpose of your assessment? What audiences will use the results? What other information will these audiences use to reach conclusions or to make decisions? The answers to these questions have serious implications for what content should be included in an assessment, how it should be constructed, and how much attention should be given to ensuring its quality.

Consequences Make a Difference

It's clear that some decisions about students and schools carry more serious consequences than others. High-stakes tests carry serious consequences. Low-stakes assessments have less serious impact on individuals. These include assessments used to monitor progress, plan instruction, even grade courses (if a variety of scores and other evidence will be used to constitute the grade). The higher the stakes associated with an assessment, the greater the need to document its quality—its validity and reliability.

Gather Corroborating Evidence for Decision Making

Even in low-stakes situations, errors can compound and cause great harm. The accumulation of your unit tests and other classroom assessments send important messages to students and parents and can have significant impact on them. Likewise, informal judgments of school quality based on assessment results can affect faculty morale and practices over time. Thus, validity warrants your attention regardless of whether your assessment context is high or low stakes.

Identifying early on whether your assessment is high or low stakes will help you determine how much evidence you need to document the quality of your assessment. What are the consequences of test performance? Will assessment results be used with lots of other corroborating information to make decisions about students? Will it be nearly the sole basis for a decision? If a score-based decision is incorrect, is it easily fixed? Could you be sued? If an assessment carries serious consequences, as do nearly all those used for accountability, placement, or funding purposes, formal evidence of validity for intended purposes is essential.

Evidence of Validity: How Do You Know an Assessment is Giving You Good Information?

Concerns for assessment validity are threaded throughout this book, so some of the issues highlighted here will sound familiar. As should be clear, the quality or validity of an assessment for a particular purpose depends on several issues and requires consideration of a variety of evidence. Those interested in greater technical detail and in techniques for gathering corroborating evidence may be interested in *Standards for Educational and Psychological Tests* (1985). These standards serve as the touchstone for test quality whenever an assessment is called into question during a lawsuit. Adhering to them provides you with some assurance that any assessment you might use that could result in litigation will be defensible.

Can the Scores Be Used To Describe What Students Have Learned?

One of the primary uses of assessment is to find out what students know or have learned with regard to particular instructional goals. Validity for such a purpose requires a good match between those goals and the content of the assessment. The following questions will help you determine whether there is such a match:

- Is the test accompanied by a clear definition of assessment goals so that you can judge the match between skills and knowledge intended for assessment and those emphasized in your class or school?

- Does the content of the assessment reflect the most important and full range of content in your curriculum? Is there a good match between the task description and your instructional priorities?

- Do the assessment tasks require the kinds of knowledge, thinking, problem-solving, and process skills that are addressed by your instruction?

- Does the assessment tap complex thinking skills? Which ones?

- Does the assessment include scoring criteria? If so, do the criteria match instructional goals, current learning theories, and curriculum priorities?

- Do the criteria include standards for judging the adequacy of student performance. If so, how were these standards determined?

- Is the task developmentally appropriate? Does it reflect processes and outcomes suitable to the intended students?

- Have students had sufficient opportunity to learn what's included in the assessment?

When you answer questions like these in the affirmative, you have some evidence that your assessment results will lead to accurate conclusions about how well students have achieved instructional goals and about how effective your instruction has been.

If you want additional evidence of the validity of your test on these dimensions, you might ask a colleague to review your assessment and either pose the same set of questions or a less directive set such as the following:

1. What do you think this assessment measures?

2. What will this assessment tell me about my students in terms of

my goals? Our school's performance standards? Important student outcomes? Student strengths and weaknesses?

3 Is this type of assessment what you would have visualized to assess my goals?

4. What might a typical response to this assessment look like?

Still more formal evidence results if you convene a panel of subject matter experts and ask them to rate your assessment on the same questions of curriculum match. For a high-stakes test, such as your state assessment, you should look for such evidence.

In reviewing your assessment for validity in these areas, be aware of the limits of "face" validity. While the task on the surface may appear to assess desired outcomes, until you see the actual student responses, you cannot be completely clear about what you are measuring. What knowledge and skills do students actually use to respond to your assessment? The only way you know whether the assessment really assesses your intended goals is to gather evidence corroborating the test score interpretation. We could collect this evidence through observation, careful review of student performance, or debriefing students about what skills and knowledge they used to address the assessment task. For example, if your assessment is designed to judge a student's ability to make connections between Hamlet's personality and other historical figures, you cannot be completely sure that the responses represent critical thinking and extension of concepts to new contexts. To know that your assessment is yielding valid results, you need to reassure yourself that students have not rehearsed and memorized answers, used some published analysis of Hamlet, or answered this question previously.

Once you determine that your assessment reflects intended goals, you can entertain the important issue of how well the particular test score typifies a student's achievement.

Are the Scores Valid for Making Generalizations About a Student?

An important issue in the validity of performance assessments for any purpose relates to whether you can generalize from a student's performance on one task to the next. After all, we teach for transfer. We want our students to possess enduring knowledge and skills. Therefore, we hope and often assume that student performance on our assessment tasks generalize to a larger domain and that the results of an assessment represent how students will perform on a larger set of tasks. After all, when we give students a hands-on science assessment involving silk worms, we probably don't care as much whether students are able to do that specific silk worm experiment as we do about their skills in using the scientific method.

This issue of transfer and generalizability appears to be a problem area in alternative assessment, where available time constrains the number of tasks that students can complete. What tasks, skills, content, and performances need to be included in an assessment to ensure that it generalizes to the larger domain of interest? How many samples of student performance do we need before we can make these generalizations? We don't know precisely, but the answer, unfortunately, is substantially more than one.

For example, Herman (1991) reviewed the research on writing assessment and found that writing skill doesn't generalize across genres. More specifically, students who write good persuasive essays don't necessarily write good stories or literary critiques. Further, even within a genre, students' performance may vary substantially depending on the topic or prompt. These findings suggest that despite the intuitive validity of performance tasks and the extent to which they meaningfully engage students, alternative assessments may not necessarily lead to more valid inferences about larger performance domains. In other words, there appears to be a trade-off between depth and breadth of information provided by such assessments.

How do we know whether the results from a student's assessment represent some larger, meaningful domain of performance? We gather evidence of generalizability by looking at the consistency of student performance across tasks that are intended to assess the same knowledge, skills, and dispositions. Technically, we can perform special statistical analyses that quantify the relationship between performance on one task and another, then use the decision rules for particular statistical tests to decide if we should have confidence in the results. While the appropriate analyses to use are well beyond the scope of this book, be aware that in high-stakes settings involving mandated tests, you want statistical evidence. Formal evidence should be presented to answer the question: Based on this one task, how accurate is my decision about a student? Or, even more useful is the question, how many tasks similar to this one must a student perform in order for me to make a decision with any assurance of accuracy?

Recognizing that it is impractical to do complex statistical analyses on most classroom assessments, we can still improve the validity of our inferences about students by using as many observations or work samples as possible before making general statements or drawing conclusions about a student's performance capability.

Can the Scores Be Used to Diagnose Students' Strengths and Weaknesses?

Can the scores be used to diagnose the strengths and weaknesses of the curriculum? Another validity issue central to classroom and school uses of assessments is their diagnostic utility. Do the results tell you anything meaningful about why students performed as they did?

If you wish to use scores to diagnose student strengths and weaknesses, the tasks and scoring criteria must be built on some credible learning theory of skill or knowledge acquisition. Let's look at what happens when a supposedly "diagnostic" score doesn't refer back to supported theory. In recent times, if a student's writing was judged to be inadequate, teachers would focus on teaching prerequisite skills such as grammar, mechanics, and paragraph structure. Research on the writing process discredits this discrete skills approach along with the diagnostic value of counting grammatical and mechanical errors as indicators of writing quality (Braddock et al. 1963, Elley et al. 1976). We can cite an analogous example in the area of mathematics. While the automaticity of calculation helps students do well in mathematics, it may be that mastery of fractions, decimals, and long division does not enhance student performance in algebra. In short, the pre-algebra diagnostic tests inflicted on most 8th grade students in this country are based on faulty theories of algebra readiness. These examples illustrate the formidable challenge in creating diagnostic assessments as well as the caution we must exercise when looking for diagnostic information from our own assessments.

In previous chapters we stressed the need to link task descriptions and criteria to current theories of curriculum and learning. This theoretical grounding also provides a link between desired outcomes and necessary prerequisites. Diagnostically valid assessment provides evidence of a body of research that supports the link between particular diagnostic scores and underlying theory.

Is the Score Unbiased?

Another critically important validity concern in classroom and school assessment is one of fairness and bias. Recent cognitive learning theory underscores the importance of background knowledge in solving problems. It's clear that students from different socioeconomic, cultural, and linguistic backgrounds may possess different kinds of prior knowledge and experience. Do students have sufficient background knowledge to engage successfully in the assessment task? Does the content or context of the assessment give unfair advantage or disadvantage to children from different cultural or language groups? Is it equally meaningful and motivating for students of diverse backgrounds? Does the assessment contain culturally insensitive material or stereotyping? Answers to questions such as these provide one line of evidence about the bias or fairness of assessments.

Problems of differences in background knowledge can be minimized if we are sure that all students have ample opportunity in school to acquire required knowledge and skills. Teachers must ensure that what is being measured has been taught and that students have had the opportunity to learn relevant content and apply desired processes. Many authorities believe that evidence of opportunity to learn ought to be collected routinely in high-stakes testing situations. We want to be sure that all students have at least had an equal opportunity to learn.

A variety of statistical analyses can be conducted to examine potential bias. Such analyses essentially look for differential performance among subgroups, controlling for various factors. While few teachers or school-based practitioners will be called on to conduct such analyses, they should be aware that such analyses exist and should be available for high-stakes, mandated tests.

Is There Corroborating Evidence that the Assessment Serves its Intended Purposes?

As should be clear at this point, demonstrating that an assessment is valid for a purpose requires gathering specific data to show the relationship between the results of the assessment and that purpose. For high-stakes, mandated tests, this means there should be specific studies investigating the meaning of the test scores (Shepard 1991). For example, if the results of a statewide mathematics portfolio assessment are used to identify school level strengths and weaknesses, then the state testing program needs to gather evidence that the scores can be used in this way. Or, if we claim that the senior portfolio, exhibition, or thesis demonstrates a student's critical thinking and expressive abilities as well as mastery of certain content, we need independent, corroborating evidence of this score interpretation. Similarly, if we use the results of an assessment to determine who gets into algebra, we need independent evidence of the relationship between the content of the test, algebra readiness, and subsequent course performance.

Does the Assessment Have Positive Consequences for Learning and Instruction?

The current controversy about traditional standardized tests should teach us an important lesson: We need to be vigilant about the consequences of an assessment. Good intentions do not ensure beneficial results. Test-based accountability was intended to help improve schools and their effectiveness with students. To many, over-reliance on multiple-choice testing has hurt the educational process and detracted from meaningful teaching and learning.

We want to make sure that our new assessments help rather than hurt schools and the people within them. For high-stakes, mandated testing programs, this means continuous attention to the actual effects of programs and formal studies to evaluate the effects on curriculum, teaching, and student learning, among other intended and unintended consequences. For a teacher in the classroom, it means attention to the effects of assessment, for example:

- What values are implied by the assessment? Does it encourage thoughtfulness and accuracy rather than impulsivity? Multiple solutions versus one right answer? Does it honor diversity?

- Is the time students and teachers spend preparing for this assessment well spent?

- Are the outcomes worthwhile? Are students held to a high standard? Does the task call for complex, rich, challenging use of students' minds?

- Are the tasks authentic and meaningful for students? Can students see connections to their own lives?

Reprise: Ensuring Reliability and Validity

To repeat, we want to have confidence in the quality of an assessment prior to using it. Figure 7.1 summarizes some of the strategies discussed in this and previous chapters that contribute to such confidence.

How Can You Use Assessment Results to Improve Instruction?

Although we've traveled an arduous path to get here, we have finally arrived with high-quality assessments, appropriate to our intended uses.

Figure 7.1
Building Reliability and Validity into Alternative Assessments

Test Development Stage	Strategies for Ensuring Valid Score Inferences
Identifying testing goals	• Link goals to important curricular objectives related to transferable or fundamental content, skills, processes • Create clear, unambiguous goal statements
Creating task descriptions	• Create fully developed task description • Review task description against goals
Selecting/ developing criteria	• Review criteria against goals and underlying learning, instructional, and/or curriculum theory • Ensure criteria reflect teachable goals • Ensure criteria don't favor a particular gender, ethnicity, language background
Scoring performances/ products/ processes	• Classroom use: score systematically and recheck work periodically • Score like topics or like dimensions at same time • Large-scale use: train raters, monitor consistency • Document the several kinds of reliability (intrarater, interrater, across topic, occasion, for students over time) • Ensure minimal levels of "reliability" (each kind that's appropriate) and a reliability coefficient of at least .70 for most assessments, .90 for high-stakes tests
Using alternative assessments	• Limit inferences from scores to the use for which the assessment was developed or for which you find multiple sources of evidence that the score can be used in a particular way • Find evidence to support score-based inferences in the test manual, research studies, from colleagues • Check inferences from test scores against other kinds of information, your prior experience, other scores, other work student does, observations • Never make an important decision based on only one score

How will we use them? Most often, we'll use assessment results to answer two basic questions:

- How are we doing?
- How can we do better?

We seek to answer these questions at any number of levels, from answers about individual students to those about the school, the school district, the state, or even the nation. For example, at the individual level: How is Kang doing in mathematics? And depending on our answer, how can we help him improve? How is Clarissa doing in science? And what does that mean about which course assignments will be of most benefit to her next year? Or at the class level: How did my students do in oral expression? What does that tell me about the strengths and weaknesses of my instruction in that area? Does a particular group or the class as a whole need remediation? Or at the school level, how did the 5th grade do in various types of writing? What do the findings suggest for the strengths and weaknesses of our curriculum and instructional materials?

In the following sections we discuss basic approaches to answering each of these familiar questions.

How Are We Doing?

Setting Standards

Implicit in "how are we doing" questions are concerns for quality and standards. We want to know not only how students are doing, but more important, are students accomplishing intended goals? Are they performing well? Are they performing as well as we expected? In a nutshell, "are we doing well—or at least okay?"

How do we determine the answer to such questions? Ideally, in formulating your scoring criteria, you also considered standards for performance. For example you decided that a "5" meant excellent and a "3" meant minimally passing. If this is the case, you can answer the "how are we doing" question by referring to the standards in your scoring criteria. If your criteria are descriptive and do not include performance levels, this is the time to equate specific score points to performance standards. There are two basic types of standards or comparisons: absolute and relative. Absolute standards hold sway when we decide how well students are doing by referring to some criterion of adequate performance. Sometimes this criterion is set formally by a school or district; sometimes it's a discipline-based standard. Mathematicians agree on what should be included in mathematics solutions. English teachers concur on standards for clearly written summaries. Social studies teachers know what evidence is acceptable in supporting a political position. We refer to these standards when answering such questions as: Was Leticia able to write an effective research report? Was Judd able to estimate the costs of establishing a new restaurant?

We can also use relative standards to judge how well students are doing. Relative standards are simply those that compare your students' performances to other groups of students. Comparing students to the national norm (for example, the score at the 50th percentile achieved by a national sample of students) is a common example of a relative standard. Experienced teachers commonly compare their students to other groups with whom they're familiar when judging student performance. They may have a pretty good idea of grade-level performance and typical student behavior based on past classes, or on comparisons with colleagues' classes, or even with the results of state and national assessment data. Relative standards help us answer such questions as: Did the new materials seem to help this year's students do better than last year's? Are John's literacy skills developing at an acceptable rate compared to developmental norms? Are students in the interdisciplinary curriculum doing as well or better than those in the regular curriculum? If it's a grade we are assigning, we often use relative standards by comparing current performance to other students' past performance levels.

While sometimes useful, relative standards have serious limitations. Their value is limited by the similarity of the groups being compared. For example, it would be unfair and inappropriate to compare the performance of special education students on a standardized test to that of a typical national norm group from which most special education students have been omitted. Likewise, the ranking of countries in international test comparisons to draw conclusions about the quality of a nation's educational system are misleading when various kinds and proportions of students take the test in different countries. The average test scores in one international assessment came from 75 percent of the 17-year-olds in the United States, but from only the top 9 percent of 17-year-olds in West Germany, and the top 45 percent in Sweden.

A word should be said here, too, on another kind of relative standard—the practice of "grading on a curve," in which teachers decide at the beginning of a class that the top portion of students will get A's, the middle will get B's, and the bottom will get C's or D's with no further definition of what level of performance is expected for each grade. This kind of relative standard merely ranks students. The problem is that although Kenny and Leila score higher than anyone else and receive A's, they may not have learned enough of the content or may not be able to perform well enough to be worthy of an A according to an absolute standard of performance quality. Likewise, if the teacher and materials are good enough, the entire class may be able to do very good work deserving of an A. The point is that while relative standards have their place, the value of absolute standards is often overlooked. Telling students you are grading on a curve suggests to them that it's enough to be better than someone else, that whoever is in the lower third is second rate, regardless of their efforts and yours, and that absolute standards of what constitutes acceptable or excellent work are not important.

Applying standards is part of the unconscious process people use to make judgments. Both absolute and relative standards present useful approaches for determining how well students are performing. In fact, absolute standards often incorporate relative information. How do we know that students have to get 80 percent correct on the laboratory procedures test to be successful in chemistry? Because from our experience, we have found that most successful students have scored at least 80 percent on the science laboratory procedures test. In most instances, you will answer the "how are we doing" question by referring both to absolute standards and appropriate reference groups.

Using Test Results To Make Decisions

Once you establish whether you wish to compare student performance to absolute standards or relative standards, you can select from several techniques for summarizing your assessment results. As you use these summary procedures, keep in mind that there is much about student performance the score does not reveal. Any summarization process creates a trade-off between economy and rich description. We believe that the descriptive information provided by alternative assessments is one of their most compelling attributes. However, there will be occasions when you will need to communicate results as numerical summaries. There are three basic ways of presenting the numbers. You can present them as a distribution of scores; by giving the average, median, or mode; or by showing the percent of students reaching some absolute standard.

How you summarize depends on the kinds of comparisons you want to make and whether your scoring criteria include only one dimension (scale) or several.

Summarizing a Single Dimension

Let's look first at the simple case, a holistic or single dimension scoring system.

Distribution of Scores

To look at the range of student performance on one dimension, simply calculate how many students received each possible score. You can even make a sketch of the score distribution, using either the raw number or percent of students attaining each score. A picture of class performance, such as Figure 7.2, shows us whether most students are scoring high, low, or somewhere in the middle. This may be particularly helpful when you have no preconceived notion of how students will perform. You can use such graphs to monitor how well you succeed with students from one year to the next. Researchers call the initial measurement "baseline information."

Figure 7.3 illustrates the distribution of student performance (on one scale) on two different history essay topics CRESST has used in research. Note that the graph shows us that more students scored higher (3.5 to 5.0) on the immigration topic than on the Lincoln-Douglas topic. What might such a finding suggest about the relative strength of instruction in these two topic areas?

Average score. Another way to look at how well students are doing is to calculate numerical summaries of class performance using mean (arithmetic average), median (half scoring above, half below), or mode (most frequently occurring score). These numerical summaries show us how the bulk of the students are doing. They provide a useful shorthand for communicating with others.

If a colleague asks how your students are doing in oxidation-reduction equations, you can use summary statistics to answer—"On an 8-point scale, they average 6.8." Your colleague can form a mental picture of where the majority of the students seem to cluster and compare that performance to her class, to last year's students, or to her understanding of what the criteria say a "6.8" student is capable of doing.

Percent-reaching standard. If you are using an absolute standard, you can decide which score point represents mastery or you might use a two-tiered standard of adequate and exemplary performance. For example, on a 5-point scale, 3 might be considered sufficient for mastery in the first system. In the two-tiered system, a score of 3 might represent adequate performance and a score of 4 or better might be required to

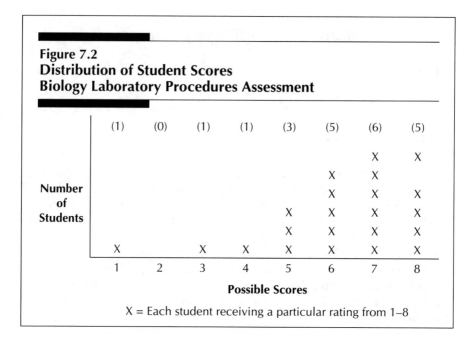

Figure 7.2
Distribution of Student Scores
Biology Laboratory Procedures Assessment

	(1)	(0)	(1)	(1)	(3)	(5)	(6)	(5)
							X	X
						X	X	
Number						X	X	X
of					X	X	X	X
Students					X	X	X	X
	X		X	X	X	X	X	X
	1	2	3	4	5	6	7	8

Possible Scores

X = Each student receiving a particular rating from 1–8

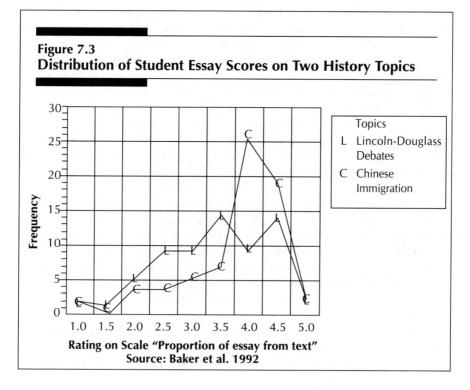

Figure 7.3
Distribution of Student Essay Scores on Two History Topics

Topics
L Lincoln-Douglass Debates
C Chinese Immigration

Frequency

Rating on Scale "Proportion of essay from text"
Source: Baker et al. 1992

reach the level of exemplary performance. Thus you might report that 10 percent of your students achieved a score of 4 or more, reaching the standard of exemplary performance and that an additional 50 percent of students scored 3, reaching the standard of adequate performance. This might be presented in a pie chart to illustrate what proportion of students fell in each category (see Figure 7.4). As with average scores, percent-mastery data from one year or group can be compared to that from another year or group.

Trends over time. Regardless of whether you look at distributions, averages, or percent of students reaching a standard of performance, you may want to keep track of trends in performance over time. You can ask yourself, "Did the same proportion of my class this year receive high scores compared to last year's class?" "Was this year's class average above or below that of last year's?" "What proportion of this year's seniors reached the 'exemplary performance' level compared to last year's?" For an individual student you might ask, "How does Justin's score on this persuasive essay compare with his September, November, and February persuasive essay scores?" These longitudinal comparisons help you put the performance of present students into perspective.

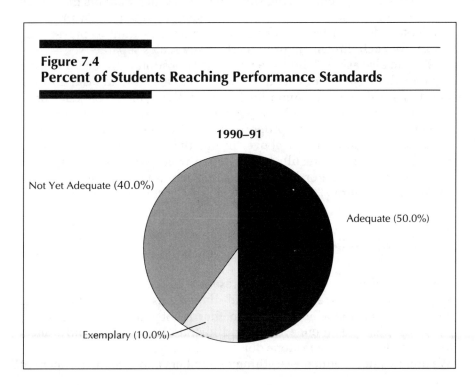

Figure 7.4
Percent of Students Reaching Performance Standards

1990–91

Not Yet Adequate (40.0%)

Adequate (50.0%)

Exemplary (10.0%)

Summarizing Several Dimensions

If you have several dimensions of performance to summarize, you have a couple of choices: (1) you can add the scores together or average them—both methods give the same overall picture of what happened, or (2) you can present separate graphs, averages, or percents for each dimension.

If you add or average scores, you may want to weight some dimensions more heavily than others if they are more important to your instructional goals. For example, although you may rate student writing on grammatical conventions, style, and coherence, you may decide to give the coherence dimension extra weight—for example, multiply these scores by 1.5 or 2—compared to grammar and style when presenting an overall summary of student work.

There are certain trade-offs involved in averaging or adding together multidimensional criteria. While you can form a general picture of student performance, you have to realize that average scores can hide widely different kinds of performance. For example, some students with an average score of 7 may have very good problem-representation skills but very poor problem-solving skills, whereas other students may score 7 on all dimensions. If you need to see such distinctions in the score results to inform instructional decisions, you may want to present the results for each dimension or for certain key scales separately.

We can also ask the "how are we doing" question with regard to each separate dimension. For example, in my math assessment task, how are my students doing in communication, in applying math concepts, or in using formulas? One useful strategy for dealing with multidimensional outcomes is to look at the proportion of subscales where student performance was adequate or above. In our three-subscale examples we could summarize our results by looking at what percentage of students received an adequate or higher rating for one dimension, for two, and for all three. Figure 7.5 provides an example of this strategy.

Samples of Student Work

Regardless of how you choose to present your findings—whether on a single dimension, average of several dimensions, or as a collection of several distinct dimensions—and whether or not you present trends over time, samples of student work help illustrate your results and inform your decisions. Numbers alone don't tell us everything we need to know. We don't want to reduce everything to numbers and lose the richness of

Figure 7.5
Summarizing Multidimensional Criteria

Percent of students rated "adequate or above" on one subscale	Percent rated "adequate or above" on two subscales	Percent rated "adequate or above" on three subscales
100%	67%	35%

student responses. More important, we don't want to lose sight of the quality of student performance and what quality work means.

In considering the "how are we doing" question, you could select performance samples that represent the best, the average, and the poorest levels of performance. These exemplars communicate clearly to other teachers and often to parents the range of performance and where particular students fit. If you keep a file of best papers or even of exemplars of poor, adequate, and fabulous, you can watch how the general level of performance for each particular group progresses. Does the excellent lab report of five years ago seem only average now? If yes, then we are doing our jobs well. Does the average group-constructed newspaper on the "Lives of the Romans" of previous years appear to be exceptional when compared with today's products? We can then conclude we have work to do. Actual performance samples can serve the same purpose as numerical summaries when making informal decisions for classroom purposes.

How Can We Do Better?

We believe the primary purpose of assessment is to provide feedback for improving individual student achievement, classroom instruction, and school programs. If after investigating individual or group results, we find we fall short of desired goals, we need to identify strategies for improvement. Diagnostic assessment identifies the kinds of changes needed if we hope to do better by looking at both the patterns and the process of performance.

Understanding Student Process

For alternative assessments to answer this "how can we improve" question, we must build into our tasks and criteria opportunities for observing and documenting student processes as well as outcomes. If we wish to understand how to help students make better group presentations, we need results related to how the presentations were planned, how roles were assigned, and how students collaborated to accomplish the task. The key to diagnosis is understanding the causes or precursors of performance. While we can never be entirely sure of what instruction causes which results, we need to consider some educated guesses, better known as hypotheses, about how adequate or excellent performance is constructed. To do this, we need to know how a specific performance is produced.

Often diagnostic information is gathered separately from the outcomes assessment. The quickest and richest source of process information is simply to watch students as they perform a task and, in appropriate circumstances, interrupt individuals from time to time to ask: What did you do to get to this point? Why did you do that? What might you do next? We can even ask students to record in journals their reflections about their work in progress; or perhaps circulate among students as they work and write quick notes for future references. Other times we might hold debriefing or in-progress conferences with students then summarize results in our anecdotal records.

At the school level, student process can be monitored in a variety of ways: (1) formal classroom observations, (2) videotaping, (3) scripting, (4) peer reviews, (5) teacher-student conferences, or even (6) document analysis, a procedure for collecting and reviewing key classroom items—syllabi, assessments, sample lesson plans, selected student work samples, and student or teacher portfolios.

We can analyze this process information by looking for patterns related to outcomes. Did successful students approach the task in significantly different ways from less successful students? What kinds of misconceptions did the poor performers hold and how might these be related to deep misunderstanding of what was taught? What kinds of errors did poor performers make? Where in the process of completing a task did students have difficulty? This ongoing feedback about how students are completing a task provides valuable information about how to help students improve.

Profiles of Performance

If you are using results from formal assessments for diagnostic purposes, they must have two characteristics: (1) a profile, scale, or set of criteria that describes component and process aspects of performance and (2) valid reasons or a theoretical framework that supports the relationship between the task components or processes and outcomes. When you have task criteria based on theoretically sound principles, you can review student performance profiles to identify areas of relative strengths and weaknesses—for individuals, groups, the class as a whole, the school, and so forth. For example, Figure 7.6 illustrates the strengths and weaknesses of Mike's history essay on the Lincoln-Douglas debate by graphing his scores on six dimensions along with the theoretical performance of an expert in history, derived from previous research at CRESST (Baker et al. 1992). Figure 7.6 suggests that compared to the history expert, Mike incorporated little overall prior knowledge and few historical principles in his essay, relied too heavily on a recently read text, constructed a relatively poor argument, and revealed several misconceptions.

When using assessment for diagnostic purposes, you want to keep in mind the relationship among the performance subscales and overall quality of performance. Your role as a diagnostician resembles that of a behavioral scientist; you are generating testable assumptions about cause and effect. What is the difference in the profiles of high- versus low-performing students? Which dimensions of performance seem to be most crucial if we want students to improve? How are the different dimensions related? Which should be taught first? For example, if your consistently excellent debaters have profiles that are uniformly high in "reference to factual information," "use of real-life examples," and "use of humor," then you would want to look at the low-performing students' profiles and see on which of these dimensions they were weakest. If you find that the poor debaters use humor and refer to real life in their arguments but are weak in the use of supporting facts, then you could begin to improve their performances by working on this skill.

At the school or district level, when we wish to strengthen instruction, our focus is on group performance rather than individuals. When reviewing group results, look at subgroups as well as subscale performance. Classroom and school level summaries often mask different kinds of prior knowledge and experiences of identifiable subgroups such as boys, girls, students new to the school, non-native English speakers,

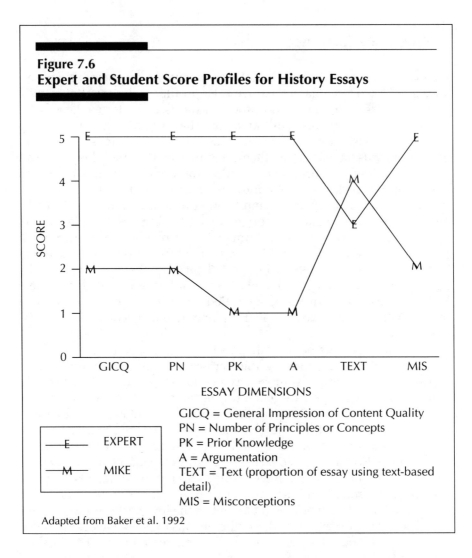

Figure 7.6
Expert and Student Score Profiles for History Essays

ESSAY DIMENSIONS

GICQ = General Impression of Content Quality
PN = Number of Principles or Concepts
PK = Prior Knowledge
A = Argumentation
TEXT = Text (proportion of essay using text-based detail)
MIS = Misconceptions

Adapted from Baker et al. 1992

students enrolled in certain courses, and so on. For example, Figure 7.7 illustrates profiles of history essay performance for boys and girls. Performance on six scales is shown, and it may be noted that girls scored higher than boys on all scales, although the difference is greater on some scales than on others. Assuming that we have ruled out differences due to rater bias, what might such subgroup differences mean for instructional decision making?

If you wish to reach all students, you will want to know if some subgroups of students have different profiles from others. For example,

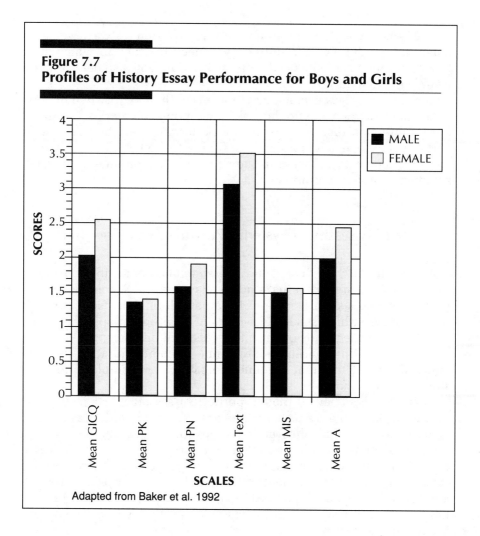

Figure 7.7
Profiles of History Essay Performance for Boys and Girls

Adapted from Baker et al. 1992

do boys and girls who score high in mathematics problem solving get this high score in the same way? Or, among the group of low-performing essay writers in your school, do students new to the school have different instructional needs from those enrolled for three or more years? Among the "barely failing" and "barely passing" scores, do we find similar or different performance profiles? Are both borderline groups similar in their ratings on grammar and language mechanics? Is there one performance dimension that separates these borderline groups, such as "organization," that can provide a focus for remedial instruction? The point here is that when you look at group results, you don't always get good diagnostic guidelines. Not only do you need to know in which areas low-performing students need more instruction, you also need to know *who* these students are.

Just as your class average may not reveal the fact that two or three students were unable to do the task at all, group summaries may give a false impression that all students are performing near the same level. Part of your diagnostic mission is to find out which students or groups are not adequately reflected in the summary and provide appropriate summaries of their performances.

The Use of Assessment Systems: Portfolios as a Case in Point

Given the limitations of using one assessment task or testing occasion to generalize about an individual student, classroom, or school, we suggest you use several tasks or occasions to gather information about a student prior to making high-stakes decisions. A longitudinal approach to assessment puts the results of any one assessment into perspective. At the same time, multiple measures of the same outcomes provide alternative views of performance that combine to create a more complete picture of student achievement.

Many teachers have turned to portfolio assessment as a strategy for creating a classroom assessment system that includes multiple measures taken over time. Portfolios have the advantage of containing several samples of student work assembled in a purposeful manner. Well-conceived portfolios include pieces representing both work in progress and "showpiece" samples, student reflection about their work, and evaluation criteria. Arter and Spandel (1992) summarize the kinds of concerns teachers should keep in mind when using portfolios or other comprehensive assessment systems:

1. How representative is the work included in the portfolio of what students can really do?

2. Do the portfolio pieces represent coached work? Independent work? Group work? Are they identified as to the amount of support students received?

3. Do the evaluation criteria for each piece and the portfolio as a whole represent the most relevant or useful dimensions of student work?

4. How well do portfolio pieces match important instructional targets or authentic tasks?

5. Do tasks or some parts of them require extraneous abilities?
6. Is there a method for ensuring that portfolios are reviewed consistently and criteria applied accurately?

Test Use: The First and Last Step in Alternative Assessment

Throughout this chapter we have discussed test use as though it were the end product of the test development cycle. But it's clear that unless test use is considered before the purchase or development of an assessment, it is virtually impossible to get the information you really need. Assessment, like instruction, requires the simultaneous consideration of many issues.

In this book, we have raised the major conceptual, if not all the technical, issues in alternative assessment. Our list is long but certainly not exhaustive. The field of alternative assessment is evolving so rapidly that today's canons are tomorrow's caveats.

Creating and using performance assessments effectively can be complicated. If this is your first introduction to it, try to absorb the big ideas first. Your assessments will probably improve, and over time the details will become more approachable as you become more comfortable with the concepts and language. Because it's an iterative process, you will revisit issues, each time with increased experience and understanding.

We hope that this guide will help you cut your way through the thicket of ever-increasing alternative assessment information so that you can find a clear pathway to more instructionally sensitive, powerful, equitable, and useful assessment.

References

Arter, J., and V. Spandel. (Spring 1992). "Using Portfolios of Student Work in Instruction and Assessment." *Educational Measurement: Issues and Practice* 11, 1: 36-44.

Baker, E.L., P.R. Aschbacher, D. Niemi, and E. Sato. (1992). *CRESST Performance Assessment Models: Assessing Content Area Explanations.* Los Angeles: University of California, Center for Research on Evaluation, Standards, and Student Testing.

Braddock, R., R. Lloyd-Jones, and L. Shoer. (1963). *Research in Written Composition.* Champaign, Ill.: National Council of Teachers of English.

Committee to Develop Standards for Educational and Psychological Evaluation. (1985). *Standards for Educational and Psychological Tests.* Washington, D.C.: American Educational Research Association, American Psychological

Association, National Council on Measurement in Education.

Elley, W.B., I.H. Barham, H. Lamb, and M. Wyllie. (1976). "The Role of Grammar in a Secondary School English Curriculum." *Research in the Teaching of English* 10, 1: 5-21.

Herman, J.L. (1991). "Research in Cognition and Learning: Implications for Achievement Testing Practice." In *Testing and Cognition* (pp. 154–165), edited by M.C. Wittrock and E.L. Baker. Englewood Cliffs, N.J.: Prentice Hall.

Herman J.L., E.L. Baker, M. Gearhart, and A. Whittaker. (1991). "Stevens Creek Portfolio Project: Writing Assessment in the Technology Classroom." *Portfolio News* 2, 3: 7-9.

Shepard, L.A., and K. Cutts-Dougherty. (April 1991). "Effects of High-Stakes Testing on Instruction." Paper presented to the annual meeting of the American Educational Research Association in Chicago, Ill.

About the Authors

Joan L. Herman is Associate Director, Center for the Study of Evaluation, National Center for Research on Evaluation, Standards, and Student Testing, University of California, Los Angeles, Graduate School of Education, 405 Hilgard Avenue, Los Angeles, CA 90024-1522.

Pamela R. Aschbacher is Project Director, Center for the Study of Evaluation, National Center for Research on Evaluation, Standards, and Student Testing, University of California, Los Angeles, Graduate School of Education, 405 Hilgard Avenue, Los Angeles, CA 90024-1522.

Lynn Winters is Assessment Director, Galef Institute, 11150 Santa Monica Boulevard, 14th Floor, Los Angeles, CA 90025.

Current ASCD Networks

ASCD sponsors numerous networks that help members exchange ideas, share common interests, identify and solve problems, grow professionally, and establish collegial relationships. The following networks may be of particular interest to readers of this book:

Authentic Assessment
Contact: Kathleen Busick, Pacific Region Educational Laboratory, Suite 1409, 1164 Bishop Street, Honolulu, Hawaii 96813. Telephone: (808) 532-1900. FAX: (808) 532-1922.

Designing District Evaluation Instruments for Math and Science Process Skills
Contact: Shelley Lipowich, Math/Science Consultant, 6321 North Canon del Pajaro, Tucson, Arizona 85715. Telephone: (602) 299-9583. FAX: (602) 886-2370.

Thinking Assessment
Contact: Sally Duff, Maryland Center for Thinking Studies, Coppin State College, 2500 West North Avenue, Baltimore, Maryland 21216. Telephone: (410) 396-9362.